Complete Book of
ZONE GAME
BASKETBALL

Harry L. "Mike" Harkins

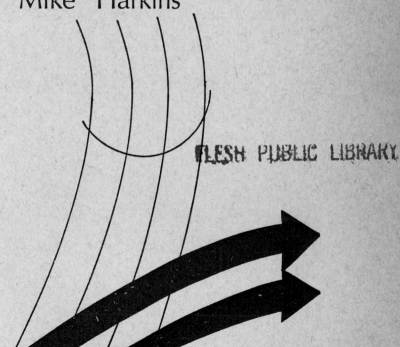

Parker Publishing Company, Inc.   West Nyack, N.Y.

©1981, *by*

PARKER PUBLISHING COMPANY, INC.

West Nyack, N.Y.

Library of Congress Cataloging in Publication Data
Harkins, Harry L
　　Complete book of zone game basketball.
　　Includes index.
　　1. Basketball coaching. I. Title.
GV885.3.H85　　　796.32'32　　　80-24541
ISBN 0-13-158709-9

Printed in the United States of America

Dedication

To Mr. & Mrs. Steve Kozy
with thanks for their patience and understanding.

Previous Books by the Author

Pressure Game Basketball
Seven Championship-Tested Basketball Offenses
Tempo-Control Basketball
Successful Team Techniques in Basketball
Coach's Guide to Basketball's 1—4 Offense

Acknowledgments

Special tribute goes to my wife, Grace, for the hours of typing (and her ability to decipher my handwritten manuscript) and for her meticulous efforts on the diagrams.

Grateful appreciation is also expressed to the sources of my basketball knowledge, including:

Russ Estey and Mike Krino, my high school coaches;
Russ Beichly and Red Cochrane, my college coaches;
The players who have played on my teams;
And the publishers of *The Coaching Clinic, Scholastic Coach, Coach and Athlete* and *Athletic Journal.*

A final note of thanks goes to my number one fans (and granddaughters), Shellee Ann and Jamee Cameron Harkins.

WHAT THIS BOOK OFFERS YOU

Probably no phase of the game of basketball causes coaches as much consternation as the zone game. The zone is no longer considered a desperation defense. It is not just something to turn to after all else has failed. It has become an accepted defensive technique that must be reckoned with. In fact, the two most widely used defenses today are the man-to-man with zone principles and the zone with man-to-man principles. This book provides viable methods of winning basketball's zone game. It includes both offensive and defensive plans.

Chapter one deals with basic ideas that should be considered when developing a zone plan.

Chapters two, three, and four give examples of specific zone offenses that provide a wide variety of techniques and are adaptable to many types of personnel. They include offenses that attempt to beat the zone with movement and offenses that utilize such new ideas as one predicated on dribble entry key plays and one based on player movement rules. Their sum total is a reservoir of ideas that should provide you with enough information to solve even the toughest zone.

Chapter five deals with the basic components of zone defenses.

Chapter six covers standard zones. These are tried and true zone defensive techniques that have proven their worth in game situations.

Chapter seven is my interpretation of Coach John Egli's famous Pennsylvania 2-3 sliding zone defense.

Chapter eight offers a complete explanation of the Monster zone defense developed at Eastern Montana College.

Chapter nine describes the check zone, the tall point man zone, and the 1-3-1 zone. All three of these zones provide methods of covering both even and odd front zone offenses.

Chapter ten deals with zone pressure defenses. It includes two new ideas: "A Two-Faced Zone Press" and "The Run and Jump Zone."

Chapter eleven starts with zone pressure offensive theory and then covers two specific zone pressure offenses: "A Guard Oriented Zone Pressure Offense," and "An All-Purpose Full Court Press Pattern."

The last chapter (twelve) gives a full discussion of the out of bounds zone game. This includes three methods of playing zone against out of bounds plays, and three out of bounds plays to be used against zone defenses.

This book is for two types of coaches: (A) It provides the young coach with the necessary background materials to formulate future zone ideas. (B) It provides experienced coaches with a measuring stick to gauge present plans, and offers some new ideas that may be added.

I feel a closeness to the defensive material in this work because my teams played nothing but zone defenses for a ten-year period. This was at a time when the zone defense was sharply criticized. Man-to-man was the defense and zones were little more than a novelty. Since that time, zones have come of age. Most of today's great teams use them at some time. For some of these teams, it is their primary defense.

On the offensive side of the ledger, there is a great need for a book on this subject. The modern zone is very sophisticated. It matches your perimeter, goes through with your cutters, double teams the corners, and does a great many other things to wreak havoc on the offense. Today's coach must have a wide variety of zone offensive techniques to fall back on. Yesterday's coach played a one-three-one offense with a baseline roamer and spent very little time on it in practice. Now he must spend almost as much practice time on the offensive zone game as he does on the offensive man-to-man game.

Coaches who read this work should find something that will help them win basketball's zone game. The zone is here to stay. If you adopt one of the techniques in total or adapt part of one to your present system and it helps you win a ball game, no one could be happier than I.

Harry L. "Mike" Harkins

CONTENTS

Contents   **15**

WINNING ZONE OFFENSE

1

This chapter deals with some basic ideas that may be incorporated into an offensive zone plan. It points out the strengths and weaknesses of zone defenses and shows what can be done to combat them. A zone offense should take into consideration the following fundamentals of zone offense.

1. FAST BREAK THE ZONE

It is a well-known fact that zones are vulnerable to the fast break game. The reason is obvious. The big zone men play in the back line of the zone. They also play under the basket at their offensive end of the court. Since they are big, it is very possible that they are slow and lack stamina. This results in a situation where the defense relies on the players who are the least able in stamina and speed to cover the most area during the phase of the game often referred to as the transition game. If the offense can bring the ball

17

up court quickly, especially after a missed shot by the opposition, they can outnumber the defense and get a good initial shot or even a second shot. Some teams increase the possibility of this occurring by screening the big opponent as he attempts to get back on defense. This is sometimes done with a small player while the offense's big man streaks downcourt in an attempt to get an easy shot.

2. SPLIT THE ZONE

Splitting the zone, or playing in the gaps, is one of the oldest and most functional methods of causing the zone problems by confusing the defensive assignments. If the defense has an odd front (1-2-2, 1-3-1, or 3-2), the offense uses an even front against it. See Diagram 1-1.

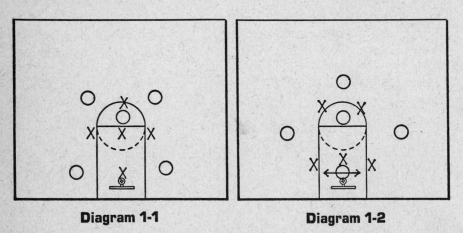

Diagram 1-1   **Diagram 1-2**

If the defense has an even front (2-1-2 or 2-3), the offense uses an odd front against it. See Diagram 1-2.

3. READ THE ZONE

Determine if it is a zone that creates pressure on the perimeter or one that simply jams the middle, and react accordingly.

Against a perimeter pressure, ball-stealing type zone, it is wise to get the ball inside.

If it is a zone that packs the middle and tries to beat you on the boards, you must pass the ball to make the zone move, take high percentage shots, and really charge the boards.

4. HOLD THE BALL AND ATTEMPT TO PULL THE ZONE OUT

This is another method of beating a tight, packed-in zone. The rules say the defense must initiate the action if they are behind or the score is tied. Make them come out and then get the ball inside.

5. HAVE A REBOUND PLAN

Despite the fact that zones are vastly improved, the heart of the zone plan is still to make you shoot outside and disallow the second shot. Some teams lose to zones because they completely overload one side of the zone and do not keep a rebounder on the offside. A team that is alert and aggressive can exploit the fact that it is difficult for zone defenders to block out. In order to get into rebound position, much time must be spent in practice to make sure that the offensive players take that extra step and make that extra move.

6. EXPECT TO TAKE THE GOOD OUTSIDE SHOTS

To prepare a team to meet a zone, the players must be made aware of the areas where shots will become available. It might be wise to designate certain areas of the floor as the zone spots and require so many shots from there each practice day. The confidence gained from regular practice from these areas might make the difference in a close game.

7. MOVE THE BALL AT A PLANNED TEMPO

The players must be taught to keep the ball moving, but at the same time to hold it long enough to exploit all possibilities. A slight fake or a single dribble may cause a defender to over-commit and thus be unable to recover in time to cover his subsequent assignment. Simply playing "hot potato" is not enough.

8. THROW CROSSCOURT PASSES

Many zones are very regimented. They are taught to make a certain slide after each particular pass. If you bypass one of your teammates and throw to another, it is a new picture for many zone players. They may under-react or over-commit and leave an area open. It is often very functional to be prepared to dribble when receiving a crosscourt pass. The eventual defender will often approach you out of control because of the length and angle of the slide he was forced to make. This may allow you to penetrate to the middle of the zone.

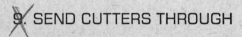

9. SEND CUTTERS THROUGH

Sending a cutter through forces the zone to tighten up in order to cover him ((1) in Diagram 1-3). It also may change the perimeter of the zone offense from even to odd.

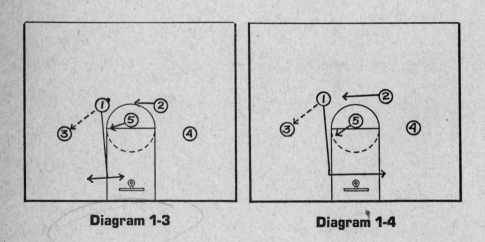

Diagram 1-3   Diagram 1-4

10. VARY THE OFFENSIVE PERIMETER

Since many zones key on the offensive perimeter, it is wise to vary it. For example, in Diagram 1-4 the offensive team starts with a two-man front, sends a cutter through, and becomes a one-man front.

If the defense was adjusting very well to this move, it might be

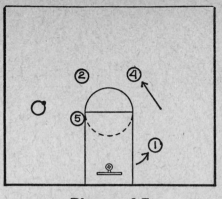

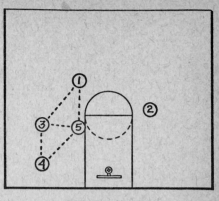

Diagram 1-5   Diagram 1-6

wise to replace the cutter (1) out front with the offside forward (4). See Diagram 1-5.

This simple move allowed the offensive perimeter to change from even to odd and back to even again with very little movement.

11. OVERLOAD THE ZONE

This maneuver consists of putting at least one guard (1), a wing man (3), a corner man (4), and a post man (5) on one side of the court and forcing the defense to cover them. If the ball is moved intelligently and the offensive triangles are utilized, a good shot is usually forthcoming. See Diagram 1-6.

12. OVERSHIFT THE ZONE

This is done by moving or faking the ball in one direction and forcing the defense to shift that way. The ball is then quickly passed in the opposite direction to utilize the fact that the zone has been overshifted.

13. SCREEN THE OVERSHIFT

An example of this type of play is shown in Diagram 1-7. The ball is passed to wing man (3). This causes the zone to shift in his direction.

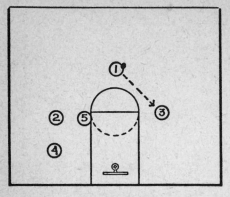

Diagram 1-7   Diagram 1-8

(2) and (5) screen the overshifted defenders, and the ball is reversed from (3) to (1) to (4) coming out of the corner for a jump shot. See Diagram 1-8.

14. TEST THE CORNER

If the ball is never passed to the corner, the zone's problems are greatly simplified. When it is passed to the corner, either the defensive big man must cover or some sort of compensating defensive maneuver must be made. If the big man covers the corner, it greatly weakens their defensive rebounding capability. If he does not, and the compensating maneuver is run, the defense must execute skillfully or the result could very well be an easy shot.

15. TEST THE MIDDLE

I read once that coaching great "Tex" Winter said he always placed a strong shooter at the free-throw line. I have always done likewise and found that this not only forced the defense to respect him, but also took some of the pressure off the perimeter.

16. GO SECOND SLIDE

A great many teams assign a front man to cover the first pass to a wing position. See X^1 in Diagram 1-9.

This keeps the three big defenders (X^3, X^4, and X^5) inside in

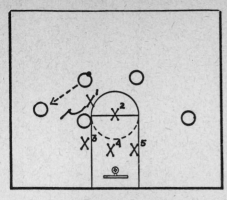 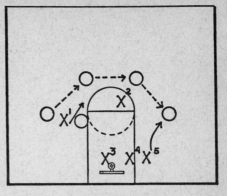

Diagram 1-9   **Diagram 1-10**

strong rebounding position. Because of this, the offense must always go second side unless a very easy shot develops quickly. By going second side, one of the bigger men (X^5) is forced to come up to cover the wing area, and the defensive rebounding potential is diminished. See Diagram 1-10.

17. TAKE ADVANTAGE OF THE PERSONNEL MATCH-UPS

A man-to-man defensive team initiates the match-ups. Their big man will cover your big man wherever he goes. Their best defender will cover your best scorer. In the zone game, the offense initiates the match-ups. You can place your big man in an area where their big man cannot cover him and place your best scorer against a weak defender. You can run the offense on a side that forces their best rebounder to come out and cover. In general, you can call the shots in regard to match-ups.

18. RUN YOUR MAN-TO-MAN OFFENSE AS A SECONDARY ZONE ATTACK

At times, the zone defense will match your offense and just seem to be able to dominate your zone offensive plan. It is wise at this time to run your man-to-man offense as a change of pace. This, of course, should be explained in practice, and potential scoring options should be pointed out. Even if the man-to-man plays are not entirely successful, they may get the defense out of its rhythm and cause your zone offense to work better when you go back to it.

19. USE THE DRIBBLE TO ADVANTAGE

There was a time when dribbling against zones was not thought to help. But in modern basketball, it is used to great advantage. It may be used to split two zone defenders and penetrate. It also may be used to rotate the zone defenders. The second use is possible because many zones play man-to-man on the ball. Thus, if the offensive man dribbles to another area, it will pull the defender out of position, and may leave a hole in the zone at the defender's original position.

20. TEACH PLAYERS TO RECEIVE THE BALL IN AN ALL-PURPOSE POSITION

An offensive player, playing against a zone, must always be aware of where he is on the court. This may require an occasional glance at the basket. He must also be aware of the direction from which the defenders will approach him when he receives the ball. Once he knows these things, he must take advantage of them by catching the ball in an all-purpose position. He must be prepared to shoot quickly, dribble past an approaching defender, or pass to an open teammate.

21. PUT A BIG MAN OUT FRONT

When your front man is tall, you can have him pass over the small front defender and into the heart of the zone. At times, a two-hand overhead pass will allow him to get the ball directly into the low post areas from the head of the key. See Diagram 1-11.

22. TEACH PLAYERS TO SLIDE INTO THE WEAK AREAS OF THE ZONE

Some players seem to have a faculty for getting open against zones. What they usually are able to do is find a spot that makes it

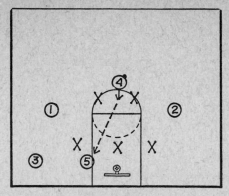

Diagram 1-11

very difficult for the zone player in their area to make his offside slides and still get back to them when the ball comes to his side. This can be taught, to a degree, by showing an offensive player what his defender is required to do both on and off the ball.

23. PASS POST-TO-POST

One of the toughest maneuvers for a zone to handle is the post-to-post pass. Very often, when a pass is made to the high post man (4), the low post man (5) is open. See Diagram 1-12.

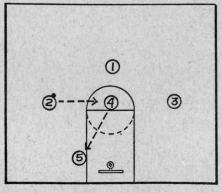

Diagram 1-12

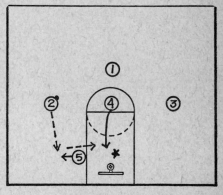

Diagram 1-13

Also, when the ball is passed to the low post man (5), if the high post man (4) will break toward the basket, he can very often receive a pass for an easy shot. See Diagram 1-13.

24. HAVE A PRESSURE DEFENSE READY

There will be nights when all of your offensive zone plans are to no avail. Have a pressure defense ready and change the tempo of the game from a rhythmic zone game to a hustling, scrambling game. A strong zone defensive team attempts to dictate the tempo of the game, and you must be prepared to counter this.

25. OVERCOME THE FEAR OF ZONES

You can do this by working against them each day in practice. Many coaches call them "cowards' defenses" or "loafer's defenses" and then lose to them on game day. Your players must come to feel that the zone is just another type of defense and that they are well prepared to meet and defeat it.

In the following three chapters are many team plans that provide methods of winning the zone game. A given offense or defense may be adopted in total, or parts of it may be incorporated into your present plan. There are techniques that suit almost every type of personnel strength and weakness. I am sure you can find a plan that suits your situation.

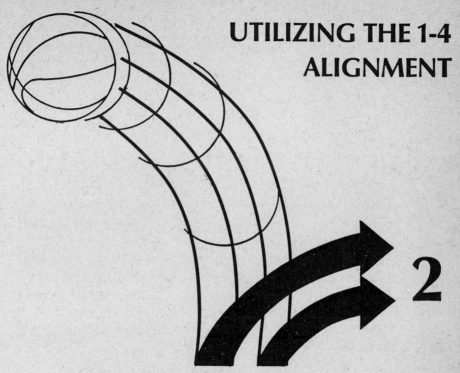

UTILIZING THE 1-4 ALIGNMENT

2

The 1-4 zone offense is very difficult to defense. Its shape makes it hard to match-up against. Diagrams 2-1 through 2-4 show how the 1-4 alignment splits the perimeter of even front zones and creates problems in the center of odd front zones. In both cases, the

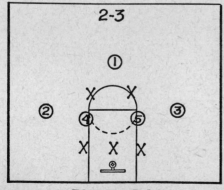

Diagram 2-1

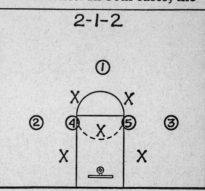

Diagram 2-2

Even Front Zones

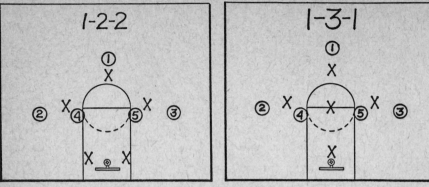

Diagram 2-3   **Diagram 2-4**
Odd Front Zones

1-4 shape causes problems for the defenders in pinpointing their specific areas of individual responsibility.

This attribute, coupled with some basic offensive zone movement, can lead to a strong zone offense. The following zone offenses are proven methods of utilizing the 1-4 alignment.

A FLUCTUATING 1-4 OFFENSE

Personnel Alignment

The initial personnel alignment for this offense includes a point man (1), two wing men (2) and (3), and two post men (4) and (5) who are located one on each side of the lane and halfway to the free-throw line. See Diagram 2-5.

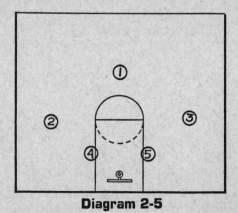

Diagram 2-5

Overshift Play

This play begins as (1) passes to (2) and cuts down and around the offside post man (5). At the same time, the offside wing man (3) moves to the front position on his side. See Diagram 2-6.

(2) looks inside for (4), crosscourt to (3), and then for (5) breaking to the high post area. If (5) receives a pass from (2), he can shoot, look for (4) inside the zone, or pass to (1), moving to the offside wing area. See Diagram 2-7.

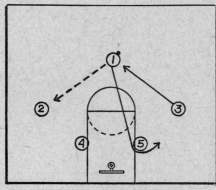

Diagram 2-6

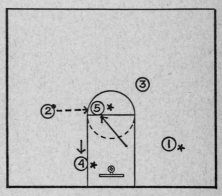

Diagram 2-7

If a pass is not forthcoming from (2), (5) moves to the ballside front area. (2) then passes to (5), who passes to (3), who passes to (1) moving to the wing position. If a good shot is available in this series of passes, it should be taken. As soon as (1) receives the ball, (5) cuts to the ballside post area. See Diagram 2-8.

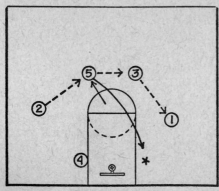

Diagram 2-8

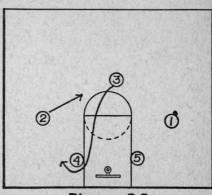

Diagram 2-9

From there, the same pattern could be keyed by (3), who could do so by cutting down and around (4). See Diagram 2-9.

Overload Play

This play begins as (1) again passes to (2) and again cuts through. This time, however, (1) would cut to the ballside, forming an overload of that side. (3) would move to the front position on his side, and the offside post man would again break to the high post area. See Diagram 2-10.

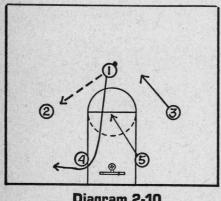

Diagram 2-10

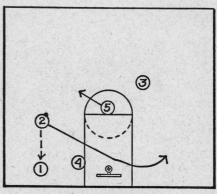

Diagram 2-11

(2) would again look for (5) in the middle or utilize the overload by passing to (1) in the corner and cutting through to the offside wing area. (5) would then move to the ballside front position. See Diagram 2-11.

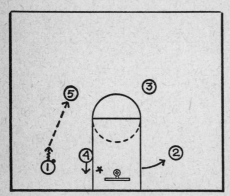

Diagram 2-12

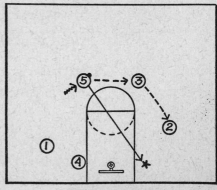

Diagram 2-13

(4) then drops low and (1) would attempt to get the ball inside to him. If he could not, he would pass to (5). See Diagram 2-12.

(5) then reverses the ball to (2) by way of (3). As soon as (2) has received the ball, (5) cuts to the ballside post area. See Diagram 2-13.

From there, (3) could cut through and call either play by his cut. A ballside cut would call the overload play and an offside cut would call the overshift play.

These two plays allow the offense to overload, overshift, check the zone's middle, and present a constantly changing perimeter to the defense.

Pass to Post

A pass to the post may be added to give the offense another dimension. When (1) passes to a post man breaking up, as to (4) in Diagram 2-14, the ballside wing man (2) cuts to his corner, the offside post man (5) cuts low by way of a diagonal cut across the key, and the offside wing man (3) attempts to find an open spot.

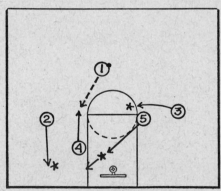

Diagram 2-14

If (4) finds no one open, he holds the ball above his head and returns it to (1). (4) then slides across the lane and, in effect, has changed sides with (5). (1) may then call the play he desires to run.

Versus Even Front Zones

It is possible to run the same plays and maintain a one-man front. This might be a desirous thing to do against an even front zone.

Overshift

This play begins as (1) passes to (2) and cuts down and around the offside post man (5). See Diagram 2-15.

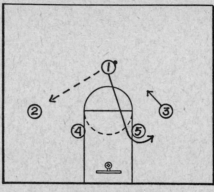

Diagram 2-15

(5) then breaks to the high post and (3) to the point. (2) can then pass the ball to (5) in the high post or reverse the ball to (1) by way of (3). See Diagrams 2-16 and 2-17.

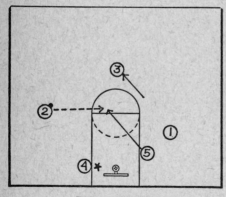

Diagram 2-16

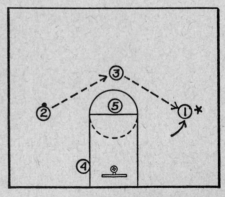

Diagram 2-17

When the ball is reversed to (1), (5) slides back to his regular post area. See Diagram 2-18.

From there, (3) could cut through and call the next play.

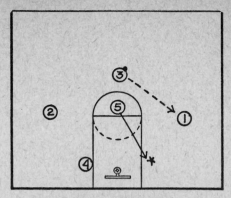

Diagram 2-18

Overload

This time, when (1) cuts through, he goes to the ballside corner to form the overload. (3) moves out front and the offside post man breaks to the free-throw line. See Diagram 2-19.

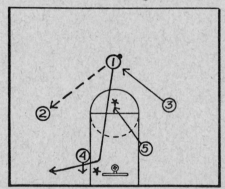

Diagram 2-19

From there (2) could pass to (5), who could shoot or look for (4) inside. (2) could also pass to (1) in the corner and cut through to the offside wing position. (1) would then dribble out and reverse the ball to (2) by way of (3). See Diagrams 2-20 and 2-21.

(5) would then swing to the ballside post area, and the offense would be reset to run another play as soon as (3) cut through. See Diagram 2-22.

The pass to the post play would be the same as previously described.

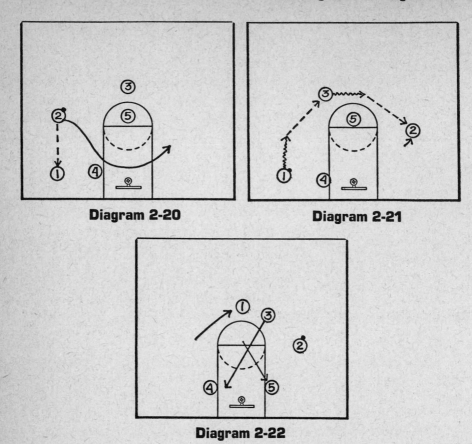

Diagram 2-20   **Diagram 2-21**

Diagram 2-22

A MOBILE 1-4 ZONE OFFENSE

This simple zone offense is designed to probe the middle of the zone, screen it, and take advantage of overload and overshift situations.

Personnel Alignment

The personnel alignment in this play consists of a point man (1), two wings (2) and (3), and two post men (4) and (5), who are as high and wide as the free-throw line.

Play #1: Pass to Wing

When (1) passes to (2), it tells the post man on his side (4) to cut to the lay-up area looking for a pass. At the same time, the offside post man (5) swings to the ballside high post area, and the offside wing man (3) cuts to the lay-up slot on his side of the court. See Diagram 2-23.

If (2) can get the ball to (5), (5) can shoot if he is open or look for either (4) or (3) in their respective lay-up slots. See Diagram 2-24.

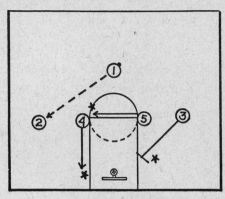

Diagram 2-23   Diagram 2-24

If the zone assignments require the middle man of the zone to come as high as the free-throw line, very often (4) or (3) will be open.

When (2) cannot get the ball to (5), he passes it back out to (1), who reverses it to (4), who has swung across the lane and around (3). (3) attempts to screen the zone and disallow it from getting out to (4). See Diagram 2-25.

If (4) cannot shoot, (5) then again breaks to the ballside and the offside wing (2) slides down to the lay-up slot on his side. From

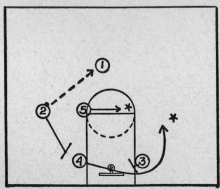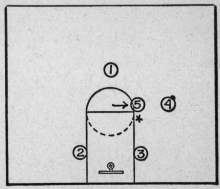

Diagram 2-25   Diagram 2-26

there, the same options are run. ((4) may pass to (5) in the middle or reverse it again by way of (1).) See Diagram 2-26.

A special option that may be worked into this continuity is called by the ballside low post man (3). In Diagram 2-27, (3) breaks three steps toward the corner and calls for the ball from (4). As soon as (3) receives the ball, (5) breaks down and will quite often split the back zone players for a power lay-up shot.

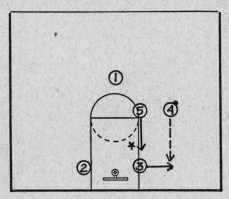

Diagram 2-27

Play #2: Dribble Overshift

This play is keyed when point man (1) dribbles at wing man (3). (3) then clears across the lane and around the offside wing man (2), who has dropped to the offside lay-up slot. The onside post man cuts to the basket and the offside post man (4) cuts to the point position. See Diagram 2-28.

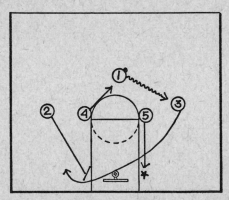

Diagram 2-28

(4) then receives a pass from (1) and may reverse it to (3), who is utilizing (2)'s offside screen.

If (3) is not open, (4) fakes the ball to him to pull the zone in that direction. This tells (1) to go down and join (5) to form a double screen for (2). (2) then comes across the lane, loops around his teammates, and receives the ball from (4). See Diagrams 2-29 and 2-30.

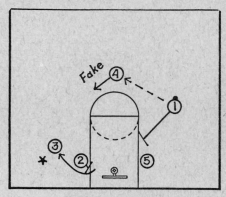

Diagram 2-29

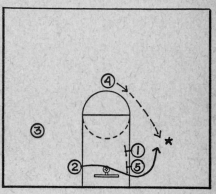

Diagram 2-30

Play #3: Dribble Overload

Again the point man (1) dribbles at wing man (3), and again the offside post man (4) comes to the point position, the offside wing (2) clears low, and the onside post man (5) cuts to the ballside low post position. But this time, (3) cuts to the ballside corner. See Diagram 2-31.

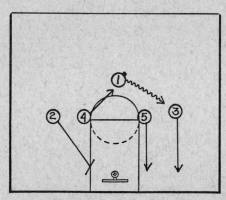

Diagram 2-31

The ball is then moved around, and the overload is utilized until the ball gets to (4) at the point. He then fakes a pass to (2) moving out to the offside wing position. See Diagram 2-32.

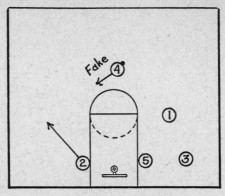

Diagram 2-32

This tells (1) to join (5) to form a double screen for (3), who pinches in then out to utilize it. (4) then may pass the ball to (3) for a jump shot. See Diagram 2-33.

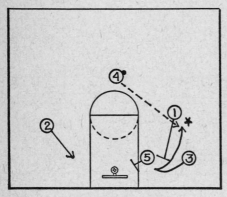

Diagram 2-33

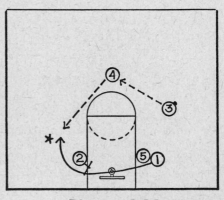

Diagram 2-34

If (3) is not open, the ball is quickly reversed to (1), who has crossed the lane and has taken advantage of (2)'s pinching screen on the nearest zone player. See Diagram 2-34.

Play #4: Pass to Post

This occurs when (1) initially passes the ball to a post man ((4)

in Diagram 2-35). When this pass is made, both the offside post man (5) and the onside forward cut deep.

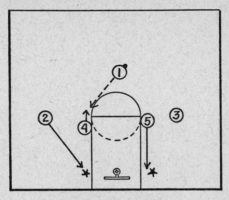

Diagram 2-35

As soon as (2) and (5) have come to a stop, the offside wing man (3) cuts to the offside high post area. (4) looks first for (2) and (5), then for (3). See Diagram 2-36.

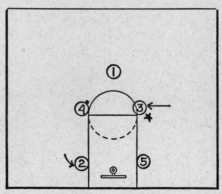

Diagram 2-36

If (3) receives the ball from (4), he looks first to shoot, then for (2) and (5), who by now have established position in their respective lay-up slots. See Diagram 2-37.

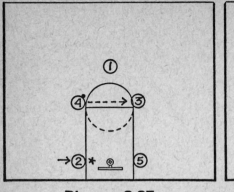

Diagram 2-37

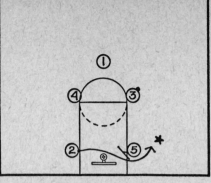

Diagram 2-38

If no one is open, (2) loops around (5), who attempts to trap the zone inside. See Diagram 2-38.

If a good shot is not forthcoming, the ball is returned to (1) and a new play is initiated. See Diagram 2-39.

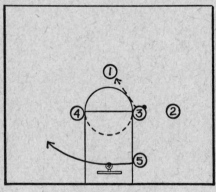

Diagram 2-39

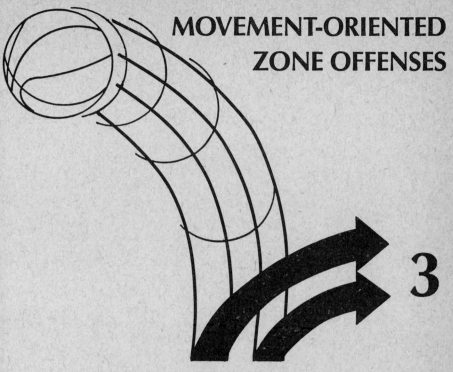

MOVEMENT-ORIENTED ZONE OFFENSES

3

For a long time zone offenses needed little movement. This was probably because of the type of zone defenses being played. The zones were rigid and, as a result, most coaches believed that against man-to-man defenses you moved the ball and the men, but that against zones the men stood still and moved the ball. It was enough to play an even front offense against an odd front zone and vice versa. Then, as zones began to rotate, fluctuate, match-up, adjust, and make many other gyrations, it became apparent that some sort of offensive zone movement was a necessity. The following movement-oriented zone offenses are examples of mobile zone offensive plays that create many problems for modern zone defenses.

A ZONE CONTINUITY

This offense attacks the zone in many ways. It tests the middle, the corners, cuts through it, screens it, and varies the offensive perimeter. It is a continuity with a natural, functional flow.

Personnel Alignment

This offense may be run from either an odd or even front. From an even front, the two guards (1) and (2) are at least as wide as the free-throw lane. The onside forward ((3) in Diagram 3-1) is as high as the free-throw line extended. The offside forward (4) is in the offside low post area, and the post man (5) is in the ballside low post area. It is preferable for the initial pass inside to be made on (3), the smaller forward's side. After this pass, the assignments of the post man (5) and the offside forward are interchangeable as the continuity is run.

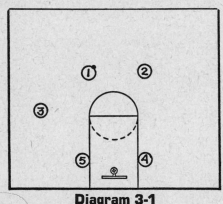

Diagram 3-1

Even Front Basic Movement

In Diagram 3-2, (1) passes to the forward on his side, (3), and the offside guard (2) cuts to the ballside high post area. Note the path of (2)'s cut. He dips down and then comes to the ball because it gives the potential passer (3) a better angle to pass him the ball. If (3) gets the ball to (2), (2) may shoot or look for (5) or (4) inside the zone.

(1) moves to (2)'s former position.

If (3) cannot get the ball to (2), (5) moves to the corner. (3) passes to (5) and cuts diagonally to the basket around (4)'s screen to the offside wing area. (4) uses (3)'s cut and comes to the ballside post area. See Diagram 3-3.

If neither (3) nor (4) are open, (2) steps out, receives the ball from (5), and reverses it to (3) by way of (1). See Diagram 3-4.

On this reversal, (1) is very often open for a shot and must be taught to be ready for it.

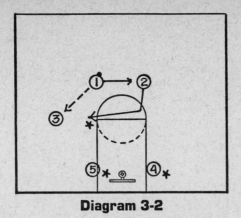

Diagram 3-2

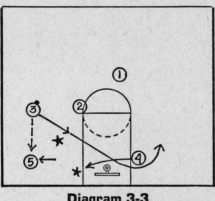

Diagram 3-3

Diagram 3-4

Once the ball goes to (3), (1) again moves away, (2) cuts to the ballside high post area, (4) and (5) move to the open post areas, and the team is in position to run the same options. See Diagram 3-5.

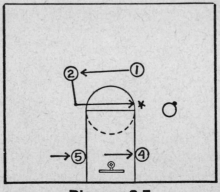

Diagram 3-5

An important coaching point should be made at this time. The players must be rebound-conscious. They must know the shot options and be prepared to charge the boards when a shot is taken. Too many teams get involved in their movement and are beaten on the boards by zone teams.

Crosscourt Pass Option

A great many zone defensive teams are vulnerable to cross-court passes. At the time (3) has received the ball from (1) and the players have cut to the positions shown in Diagram 3-6, a very functional crosscourt pass may be thrown.

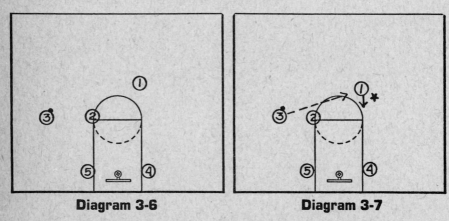

Diagram 3-6   Diagram 3-7

The defense is very concerned with jamming the high post area to prevent a pass to (2). If (3) will throw to (1), he will very often be open. See Diagram 3-7.

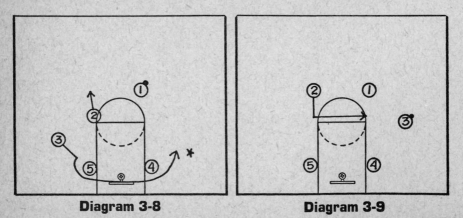

Diagram 3-8   Diagram 3-9

If (1) is not open, (2) steps back out front, (3) loops down and around (5) and (4), and (1) can pass back to (2) or to (3) as he comes around (4). See Diagram 3-8.

Once the ball gets to (3), the continuity is resumed. See Diagram 3-9.

Odd Front Basic Movement

This offense can also be run from an odd front. The shape of the offense would be 1-2-2 with (1) at the point, (2) and (3) at the wings, and (4) and (5) in a double low post. See Diagram 3-10.

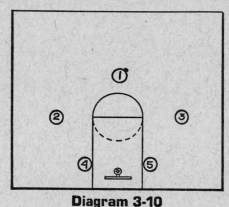

Diagram 3-10

Then on a pass from (1) to one of the wings ((2) in Diagram 3-11), the offside wing would cut to the ballside high post area. From there, the movement would be practically the same as when it was started from an even front. See Diagrams 3-12 through 3-14.

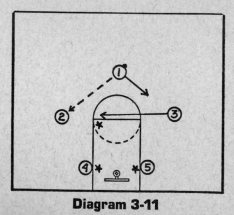

Diagram 3-11

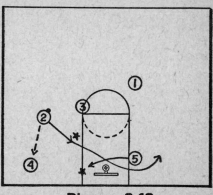

Diagram 3-12

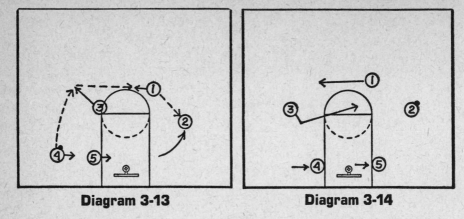

Diagram 3-13   **Diagram 3-14**

This offense combines many of the basic zone-testing components. It works against both odd and even front zones. The important caution that was made earlier should be repeated. When running a movement-oriented zone offense, much practice time must be spent on rebounding assignments.

AN OVERLOAD CONTINUITY

The following zone offense is a simple three-play plan, but provides the offensive team with overshifting moves, overloading moves, screens, and middle-testing techniques. All three plays start from a 2-1-2 formation.

Personnel Alignment

This offense begins with the two guards (1) and (2) as wide as the free-throw lane, the two forwards (3) and (4) as high as the free-throw line extended, and the post man (5) at the center of and above the free-throw line. It might be wise to have the larger guard initiate most of the play because he must cut inside. This would keep the smaller guard out front and responsible for defensive balance.

Play #1 (Keyed by Guard-to-Forward Pass)

Guard (1) passes to his forward (3) and cuts through to the ballside corner. The post man (5), who starts at a center high post position, swings to the ballside. This creates an overload on that side. See Diagram 3-15.

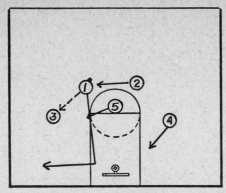

Diagram 3-15

Post man (5)'s rule is to stay between the ball and the basket. When the ball is passed to (1) in the corner, (5) slides to the low post position. Many times, when a defender goes to cover (1) in the corner and (5) slides down, the trailing defender (X⁵ in Diagram 3-16) will get too far behind him. This will leave (5) open as he slides down.

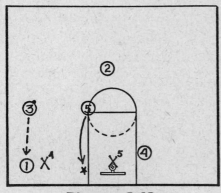

Diagram 3-16

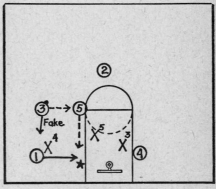

Diagram 3-17

If (3) chooses to pass to (5) in the high post, (1) can often get open by going baseline. It is almost like backdooring the zone. See Diagram 3-17.

(3) may choose to switch the overload to the other side of the court. He does this by passing to (2) at the point and cutting through to the offside corner. (2) reverses the ball to (4), (5) swings to the ballside post, and (1) replaces (3) at the now offside wing. See Diagram 3-18.

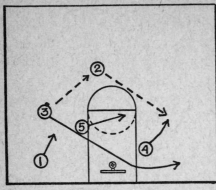

Diagram 3-18

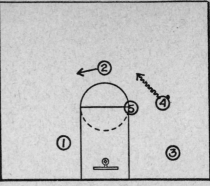

Diagram 3-19

From here, the same options may be run. Anytime a wing man on the strong side wants to return the offense to a two-man front, he dribbles to the front and the offense may be initated again. See Diagram 3-19.

Play #2 (Keyed by Guard-to-Guard Pass and Cut Through)

Guard (1) passes to guard (2), cuts around the high post man (5), and runs at the forward on that side (4). This clears forward (4) to the far corner. See Diagram 3-20.

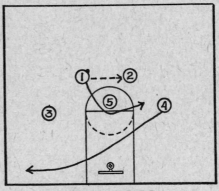

Diagram 3-20

Guard (2) takes a dribble toward the overloaded side and then passes to (1). This tells the offside wing (3) to come to the ballside low post area. When (3) arrives, (5) swings to the ballside high post area. See Diagram 3-21.

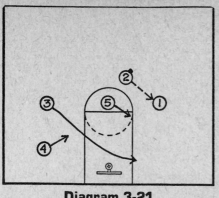
Diagram 3-21

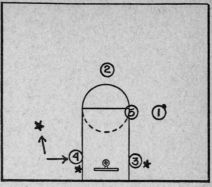
Diagram 3-22

(1)'s first option is to get the ball to (5). If he does, (5) may shoot, look for (3) inside the zone or for (4). (4) has the option of playing in tight on the lane or moving up to wing position. See Diagram 3-22.

If (1) cannot get the ball to (5), (3) moves to the ballside corner. (1) may then pass to (3) (who would shoot and look for (5) sliding down) or return the ball to (2). See Diagram 3-23.

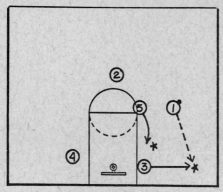
Diagram 3-23

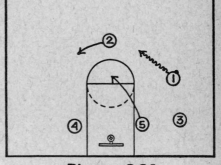
Diagram 3-24

At this point, (1) could dribble out front and return the offense to a two-man front set. See Diagram 3-24.

Play #3 (Special Situation)

This play may take place any time the ball is at the wing position on the overloaded side. In Diagram 3-25, wing man (3) calls out "2!" He then passes to the point man (1), and he and the post man (5) form a double screen on the overshifted zone. Point man (1) sets up the double screen by taking a dribble toward the farside and pulling the zone in that direction. (2) utilizes the double screen by pinching in and cutting closely off it. If (2) is open, (1) passes him the ball.

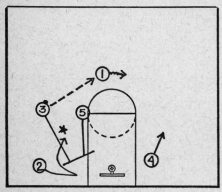
Diagram 3-25

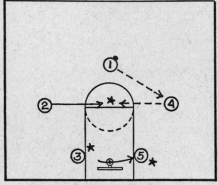
Diagram 3-26

In the event (2) is not open, (1) passes to (4), (5) swings to the ballside low post and (2) cuts into the middle high post area. If (4) can get the ball to (2), (2) may shoot or look for either (5) or (3) inside the zone. See Diagram 3-26.

If (4) cannot get the ball to (2), (2) continues to the ballside corner and the offense goes on. See Diagram 3-27.

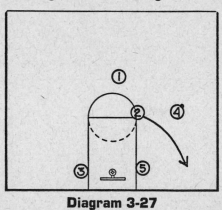
Diagram 3-27

If (4) desires, he may dribble out front. This would return the offense to a two-man front and allow either of the first two basic plays to be run.

AN ADJUSTABLE ZONE OFFENSE CONTINUITY

There are two moments of truth when you are testing a zone defense. One occurs when the ball goes to the corner, and the other occurs when the ball is passed to the center of the free-throw line. The following offense is based on probing those vital areas.

Personnel Alignment

This offense is also run from a two-guard set. It would be advisable to have the smaller guard initiate most plays because the offside guard goes inside, and the initial passer is responsible for defensive balance.

Versus One-Man Front Zones

The initial set of this offense is 2-3. (1) and (2), the two guards, are as wide as the free-throw lane. The post man (5) is in the center of the free-throw line area, and the forwards (3) and (4) are on their respective sides and are halfway to the free-throw line high. See Diagram 3-28.

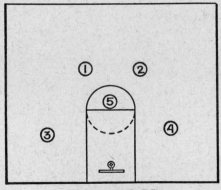

Diagram 3-28

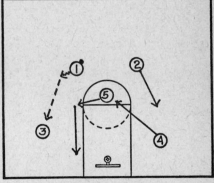

Diagram 3-29

The movement begins as (1) passes to (3), the forward on his side. This causes (5) to swing to the ballside and then down the lane looking for a possible pass from (3). At the same time, the offside forward (4) moves to the area formerly held by (5), and the offside guard (2) slides down almost to the free-throw line. See Diagram 3-29.

From here, the following four basic options are looked for:

A. If (3) can get the ball to (4), (5) may be open under the basket. See Diagram 3-30.

B. If the ball can quickly be reversed to (2), he may be open. This may be done by way of (4) or (1) (See Diagram 3-31.) or by a crosscourt pass from (3) to (2). See Diagram 3-32.

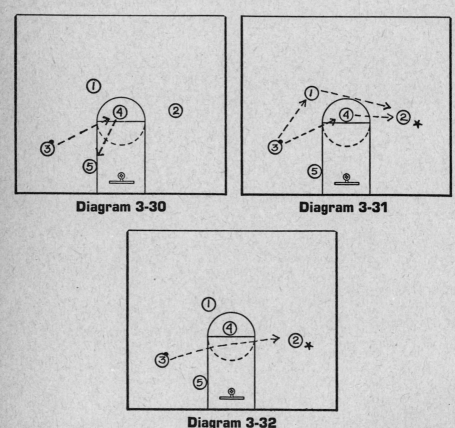

Diagram 3-30   **Diagram 3-31**

Diagram 3-32

C. If the ball is passed from (3) to (5), (4) can very often get open by sliding down from his high post location. See Diagram 3-33.

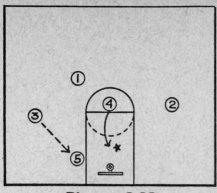

Diagram 3-33

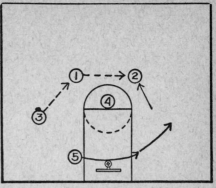

Diagram 3-34

D. If (3) desires to turn the offense over, he passes to (1), who passes to (2) moving up and toward him. At the same time, (5) swings across the lower lane area and then up, to become the onside forward. See Diagram 3-34.

On the pass from (2) to (5), (4) swings across the high post area and then down the lane, and the offside forward (3) cuts to the high post area. See Diagram 3-35.

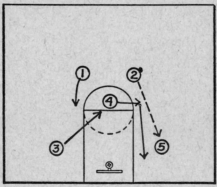

Diagram 3-35

From here, the four basic options again prevail.

Versus Two-Man Front Zones

The play starts from the same initial 2-3 set.

When guard (1) notices the opposition is in a two-man front

zone, he cuts through after his pass to his forward (3) and comes out at the far wing position. (5) still cuts to the ballside and down the lane. The offside forward (4) cuts to the high post. See Diagram 3-36.

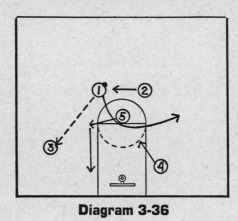

Diagram 3-36

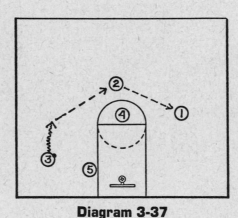

Diagram 3-37

(3) checks the four basic options and decides to reverse the ball to the other side. He does this by dribbling free-throw line high and then passing to (2), who reverses the ball to (1). See Diagram 3-37.

This causes (5) to swing across the lane to the ballside corner and (4) to move across the high lane. See Diagram 3-38.

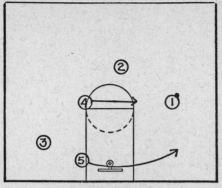

| **Diagram 3-38** | **Diagram 3-39** |

(1) then passes to (5) in the corner and again cuts through to the offside wing area. (4) slides down the lane and (3) takes the high post. See Diagram 3-39.

From here, the four basic options again prevail.

The only real difference between the offense when used against an even front is the play of the guards. (2) stays at the point and (1) changes sides each time he passes to the corner. The play of the three inside men is the same against even and odd front zones. This gives the team the ability to play in the gaps against any type of zone and still have a functional movement inside that probes the zone in the corner and in the middle.

THE ZONE POWER CONTINUITY

This offense is based on two basic zone offense fundamentals: get a good shot and have a rebound plan.

Personnel Alignment

It helps if one of the two guards (1) and (2) is a strong rebounder. Both start in basic 2-3 offensive positions, but one of them always cuts through before a shot is taken. The three inside men, (3), (4), and (5), are interchangeable. This offense would work best for a team that has forwards with inside ability fairly close to that of its center. A team with a tall pivot man and short forwards would not benefit from this offense. See Diagram 3-40.

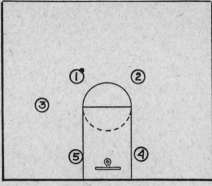

Diagram 3-40

This offense has a basic continuity in the context of which many options occur. The movement begins when a guard (1) passes to the forward on his side and then cuts through to the ballside high post area, stopping above the free-throw line. The offside guard (2) then moves toward the ballside. Post man (5) then moves about halfway to the corner. See Diagram 3-41.

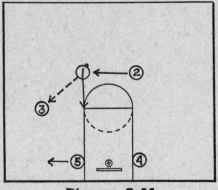

Diagram 3-41

Play #1: Pass to Point

(3) may then pass to either (2), (1), or (5). The pass that best demonstrates the continuity is the pass to (2). When this occurs, the offside forward (4) moves up to the wing area on his side, and (2)

reverses the ball to him. (3) then cuts through to the ballside low post area, (1) moves out front, and (2) cuts to the ballside high post area. See Diagram 3-42.

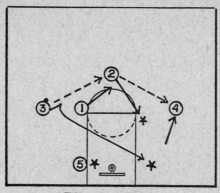

Diagram 3-42

The offense has now changed sides, and the team is in position for the three options to be run again. (4) may pass to (3) moving halfway to the corner, (1) in the high post area, or turn the offense over again by passing to (1), who is now at the point position. See Diagram 3-43.

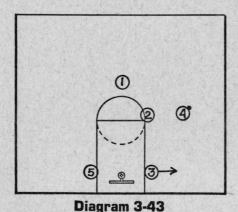

Diagram 3-43

Special Option: Overshifted Screen

During this phase of the continuity (pass to point), a couple of special scoring options may be run. For example, using the personnel as they are in Diagram 3-43, after the ball is passed to the point man, (1) would make an exaggerated fake to the offside wing man (5). This would pull the zone in that direction. Then (4) would come down and screen the overshift, and (3) would use the screen to move to the wing to receive a pass from (1) for a jump shot. See Diagram 3-44 and Diagram 3-45.

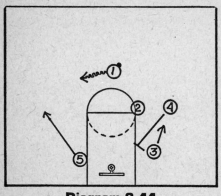

Diagram 3-44

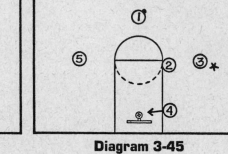

Diagram 3-45

If (3) was not open, (1) would pass the ball to (5) and cut to the high post, (4) would come across, (2) would move out front, and the offense would again be in position to run either of the three basic plays. See Diagram 3-46.

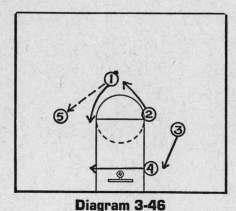

Diagram 3-46

This option can also be run against man-to-man defenses.

Special Option: Offside Screen

During this same play #1 movement, another scoring option may be added. Using the personnel alignment of Diagram 3-46, when the forward with the ball, (5), passes to the guard at the point, (2), he may rub off the guard in the high post area, (1), on his cut to the ballside low post area. See Diagram 3-47.

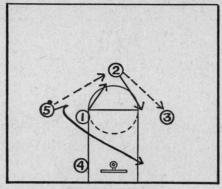

Diagram 3-47

Although this is primarily a man-to-man option, it is very useful if the offense is changing defenses or disguising its defense so well that the team cannot identify whether it is man-to-man or zone.

Play #2: Pass to High Post

Using the personnel alignment of Diagram 3-48, this play is keyed when the ballside forward (3) passes to the guard who cut to the high post area, (2). (2) may shoot or pass to either (5) or (4) inside the zone in the low post areas. This is a power play because it usually provides a good shot and a rebounding triangle. See Diagram 3-48.

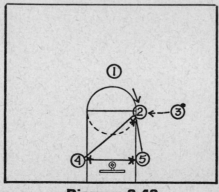

Diagram 3-48

If no one was open, (4) would break to the wing position and (2) would pass the ball to him. The offense would then change sides again. See Diagram 3-49.

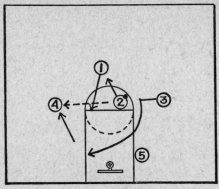

Diagram 3-49

Play #3: Pass to Low Post

Using the personnel alignment shown in Diagram 3-49, the pass to the low post play is also a power play because it provides a good shot and a rebound triangle. As (3) moves halfway to the corner, (4) passes him the ball. In many cases, (3) will be open because the wing man on that side went up to cover (4). As soon as (3) receives the ball, he looks for a shot. (4) moves to the ballside lay-up slot to form a rebound triangle along with (1) at the apex and (5) on the other side. See Diagram 3-50.

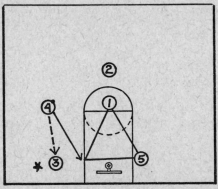

Diagram 3-50

If (3) cannot shoot, he looks for (4) cutting through and then passes to (2) out front. The two must move toward each other in order for this pass to be made. See Diagram 3-51.

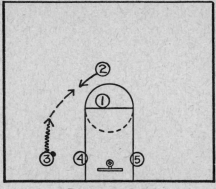

Diagram 3-51

(2) then takes the ball to (5)'s side as (5) moves to the wing position. (2) passes to (5), (4) comes across the lane, (2) then cuts to the ballside high post area, and (1) moves out front. See Diagram 3-52 and Diagram 3-53.

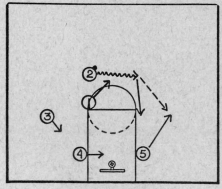 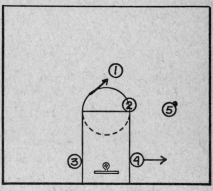

Diagram 3-52　　　　　　**Diagram 3-53**

From here, any of the three plays may be run.

This offense is easy to run, checks the zone's corner and middle, and in spite of the amount of movement, the players stay in their areas of strength. It is also a strong rebounding offense because of the built-in triangles and may be adapted to work against man-to-man defenses.

NOVEL IDEAS IN ZONE OFFENSE

4

This chapter presents three novel ideas in zone offense. "A Rule Zone Offense," "The Dribble Entry Zone Offense," and "A Box-and-One Zone Offense" offer ideas that will cause zone defenses new problems.

A RULE ZONE OFFENSE

Matching, adjusting zones very often key on the offensive guards. Basically, they are prepared to cover either an overload with a one-man front or a balanced 2-1-2 set. This offense has a two-man front and also overloads. It also provides for offside rebounding in spite of the fact that it has a two-man front and an overload. The individual players have a set of rules that allow these things to be accomplished.

The Rules and Personnel Alignment

(4) is the baseline roamer and always stays in a vertical line with the ball. He must of course, respect the three seconds in the lane rule.

(1) is always out front and is responsible for defensive balance.

(5) is the post man and stays between the ball and the basket.

(2) and (3) play on either side of (1). They are either at a strong-side wing position or at the weak-side second guard position. See Diagram 4-1.

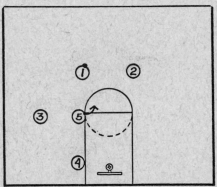

Diagram 4-1

   A. *Strong-side Wing*
They must trail (1) when he moves away from them. This converts them to the second guard position.

   B. *Weak-Side Second Guard*
When they are at the second guard position, they must stay on a horizontal line with the ball and must charge the board very hard when a shot is taken. They also will initiate changes of sides.

Rules in Action

In Diagram 4-2, (1) has the ball and passes it to (2) in the second guard position.

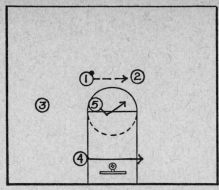

Diagram 4-2

Please note that (5) slid over and stayed between the ball and the basket, and (4) slid over to stay on a vertical line with the ball. In the event (2) would pass to (5), (4) could very well be open under the basket.

In Diagram 4-3, two passes were made. Note that (5) stayed between the ball and the basket, (4) kept his vertical line with the ball, and the second guard (2) stayed on a horizontal line with the ball. If (3) would pass to (5), (4) might have been open in the low post or (2) on the offside wing.

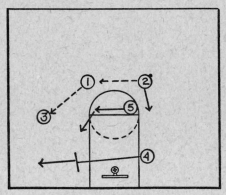

Diagram 4-3

In Diagram 4-4, the ball is passed from wing man (3) to base-line roamer (4) in the corner. Note that (2) slid all the way down to stay on a horizontal line with the ball, and (5) slid to the low post to stay on line with the ball. (4) looks first for (5) inside and then back to (3).

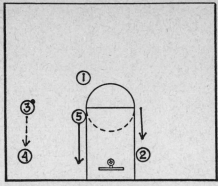

Diagram 4-4

Change of Sides

A change of sides may be initated in two ways:

A. *Second Guard Dribble*. When the ball gets to (2) in the second guard position, he can dribble to the unoccupied wing. This would cause (1) to follow him and (3) to move to the offside second guard position. See Diagram 4-5.

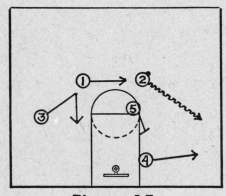

Diagram 4-5

Note that the baseline roamer (4) stayed on a vertical line with the ball, the post man (5) remained between the ball and the basket, and the now offside or second guard (1) dropped down to stay on a horizontal plane, even with the ball.

B. *Pass to Weak Side*. In Diagram 4-6, the offside guard (3) is down at the wing position because (2) has the ball. Ordinarily, when (2) passes to (1), (3) would come out front to remain in line with the ball. But, in this case, (3) breaks out to the wing position and receives a pass from (1).

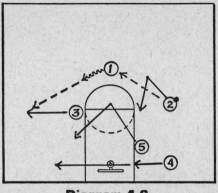

Diagram 4-6

(4) slides to the corner, (1) to his near guard area, (2) to the second guard area and then down to stay on line with the ball, and (5) moves to the ballside post. See Diagram 4-7.

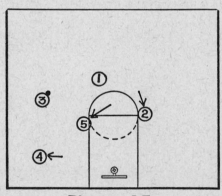

Diagram 4-7

This offense is very easy to learn. The players soon become very aware of where their teammates are. It also gives the team the ability to overload the zone, hit the post and then the man underneath, and also change sides when needed.

A DRIBBLE ENTRY ZONE OFFENSE

This zone offense is very versatile. It allows a team to overload the zone, attempt to overshift the zone, and also checks the two vital areas of the zone, which are the corner and the high middle. It consists of two basic plays that may be run consecutively.

Personnel Alignment

The initial personnel alignment consists of a point man (1), one wing man (3), a man in the high post area (2), and two post men (4) and (5). The positions of (1), (2), and (3) are interchangeable, as are those of (4) and (5). See Diagram 4-8.

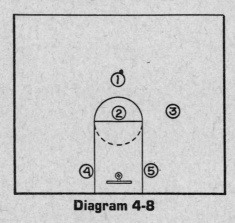

Diagram 4-8

Play Keys

As (1) dribbles upcourt, he may move toward either wing position. He may dribble toward (3). See Diagram 4-9.

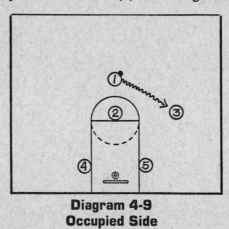

Diagram 4-9
Occupied Side

This is the key to play #1 and is called the occupied side.

He may also dribble to the unoccupied wing area on the other side. See Diagram 4-10.

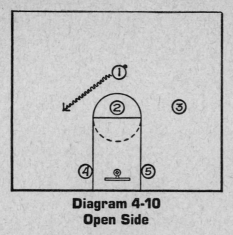

Diagram 4-10
Open Side

This is the key to play #2 and is called the open side.

Play #1 Occupied Side

When (1) dribbles at (3), it tells him to clear. He, (3), may clear to the ballside corner or to the far wing area. In either case, (2) moves from the high post area to the point to replace (1).

Option A: Overload

In Diagram 4-11, (3) clears to the ballside corner. This overloads that side of the court.

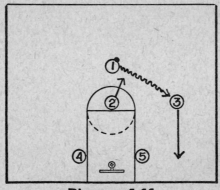

Diagram 4-11

This overload is maintained, and the ball is moved around the perimeter until (3) decides to reset the offense. He does this by cutting to the wing position on the other side of the court. The ball is then quickly reversed from (1) to (3) by way of (2). There is a chance (3) might be open because (4) attempts to screen the zone and disallow it to shift over and cover (3). See Diagram 4-12.

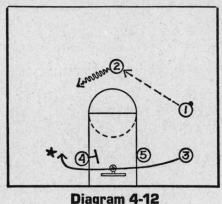

Diagram 4-12

As soon as (2) passes to (3), (1) cuts to the middle, and the team is in position to run another play once the ball has been returned to (2) at the point. See Diagrams 4-13 and 4-14.

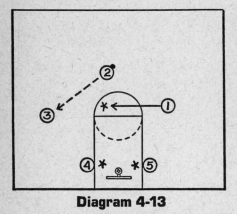
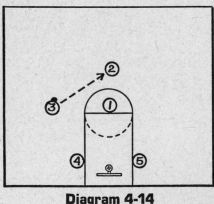

Diagram 4-13   **Diagram 4-14**

Option B: Overshift

In this case, when (1) makes his dribble entry on the occupied side, (3) clears quickly to the offside. The ball is then reversed quickly to him from (1) by way of (2), who has again stepped to the point. See Diagrams 4-15 and 4-16.

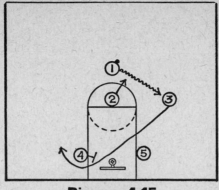

Diagram 4-15

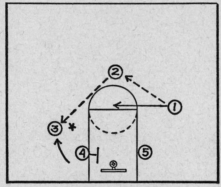

Diagram 4-16

Note that (1) cuts to the middle, and once the ball is returned to the new point man (2), another play may be keyed. See Diagram 4-17.

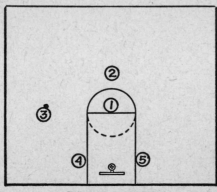

Diagram 4-17

Play #2: Open Side

In this play, the original point man (1) chooses to dribble to the open wing area. (2) again steps out front to replace him. This opens up the middle for the offside big man (5) to break into this hole. See Diagram 4-18.

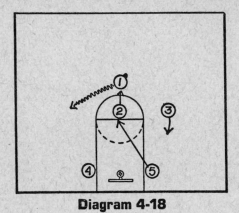

Diagram 4-18

From there, several options may occur.

Option A: High Post Pass

If (1) passes to (5), he may shoot, look for (4) inside the zone, or for (3) in the offside wing area. See Diagram 4-19.

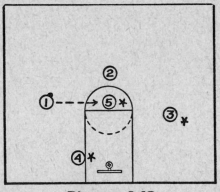

Diagram 4-19

If the ball is not passed inside, (4) clears to the offside and (5) slides down. See Diagram 4-20.

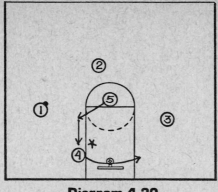

Diagram 4-20

(1) looks for (5) sliding down and then for (3) breaking into the high post area. If (3) gets the ball, he can shoot or look for (4) or (5) inside the zone. See Diagram 4-21.

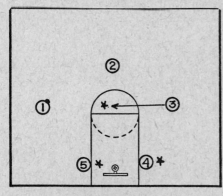

Diagram 4-21

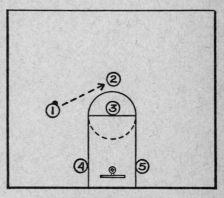

Diagram 4-22

If (1) cannot get the ball to (3), he passes to (2) out front and the team is in position to run another play. See Diagram 4-22.

This Option A is the primary objective of the play. Others that may occur if (1) cannot get the ball to the high post are as follows.

Option B: Low Post Pass

If (1) cannot get the ball to (5), he looks for (4) in the ballside low post area. When the ball is passed to (4), (5) breaks down. (4) looks first to shoot and then for (5). See Diagram 4-23.

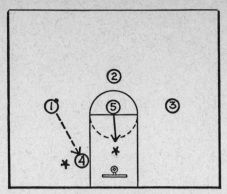

Diagram 4-23

If nothing develops from this, the ball is returned to (1), and (3) breaks to the middle. If (3) gets the ball, (4) or (5) may be open inside the zone. See Diagram 4-24.

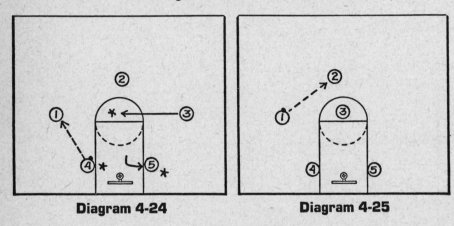

Diagram 4-24   **Diagram 4-25**

If (3) cannot receive the ball, it is passed to (2) at the point and a new play is keyed. See Diagram 4-25.

Option C: Corner Play

Once (5) has broken to the high post and cann.t get the ball from (1), (4) must clear. In this Option, he clears to the ballside corner. This creates an overload and leaves a hole in the low post area for (5) to slide down into. See Diagram 4-26.

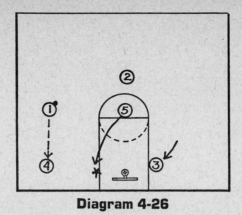

Diagram 4-26

Note that when (4) cleared to the corner, (3) dropped down to aid in rebounding.

This overload is maintained until the ball is reversed to (3). This tells the post men (4) and (5) to return to their original positions. (1) then cuts to the middle, the ball is passed to (2) at the point, and either play may be run again. See Diagram 4-27 and 4-28.

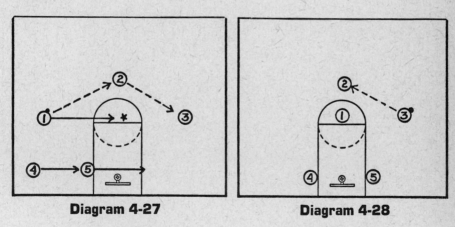

Diagram 4-27   **Diagram 4-28**

THE DRIBBLE ENTRY ZONE OFFENSE AS A FIVE-MAN INTERCHANGEABLE CONTINUITY

If the right personnel are available, a variety of this offense may be run that is, in effect, a five-man interchangeable continuity.

Open Side

When point man (1) dribbles to the open side, and the offside post man (5) breaks to the high point, then offside wing man (3) drops down to replace (5). If (5) receives the ball from (1), he may shoot or pass to (4) or (3) inside the zone. See Diagrams 4-29 and 4-30.

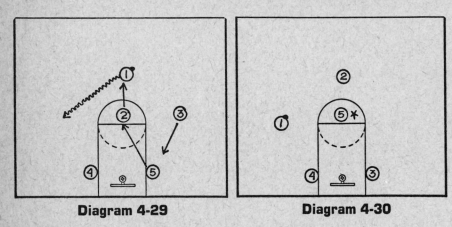

Diagram 4-29   **Diagram 4-30**

If the ball cannot be passed to (5), it is passed out front to (2), who may run either play. In Diagrams 4-31 and 4-32, he chooses to repeat the dribble to the open side.

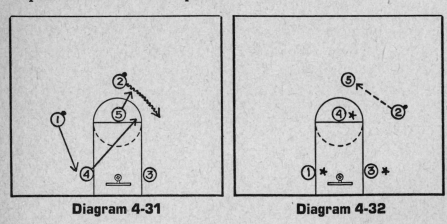

Diagram 4-31   **Diagram 4-32**

Since (2) could find no one open, he returned the ball to (5) at the point.

Occupied Side

(5) may now run either play. He chooses to dribble to the occupied side. This clears (2), and he may go to the ballside corner (see Diagram 4-33) or to the offside wing area (see Diagram 4-34).

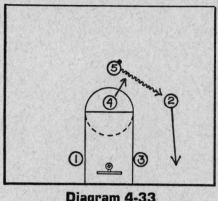

Diagram 4-33

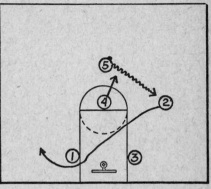

Diagram 4-34

Whatever (2) decides to do, once he has gotten to the offside wing area and the offense is balanced, the offside post man (2) will break to the high post area. See Diagram 4-35.

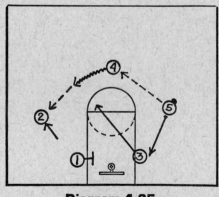

Diagram 4-35

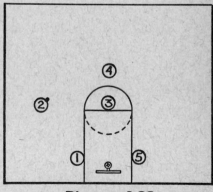

Diagram 4-36

Note that (5) dropped down to replace (3). Once the ball is returned to (4), either play may again be run. See Diagram 4-36.

Diagram 4-37 through 4-43 show this continuity in operation.

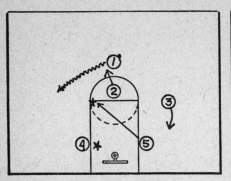

Diagram 4-37
Dribble to open side

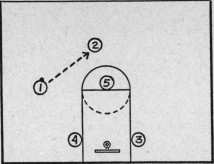

Diagram 4-38
Back out front

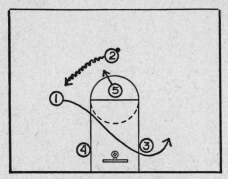

Diagram 4-39
Dribble to occupied side.
(3) cuts only after the
offense is balanced

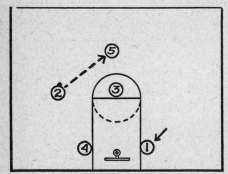

Diagram 4-40
Back out front

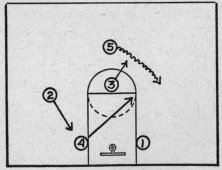

Diagram 4-41
Dribble to open side

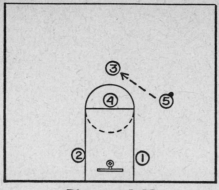

Diagram 4-42
Back out front

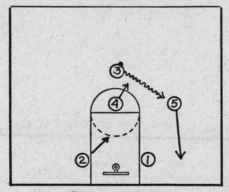

Diagram 4-43
Dribble to occupied side

It should be re-emphasized that since this continuity brings the post man out front and takes the point man inside, it can be utilized only by teams with a particular type of personnel. All five players must be able to function inside and out. Also, it must constantly be pointed out that the point man, regardless of who he is, is responsible for defensive balance.

A BOX AND ONE ZONE OFFENSE

Years ago, zone offense was simplified with the use of a 1-3-1 offense that utilized a baseline roamer. This same basic concept can be adapted to a box formation with a baseline roamer.

Personnel Alignment

The beginning personnel lineup consists of two guards (1) and (2), two post men located one in each low post area, and a very strong shooter (3) roaming the baseline. (3) should try to be in the ballside corner. He can be helped to do this by (1) and (2) if they are aware of his position and attempt to get the ball to him. See Diagram 4-44.

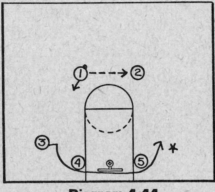

Diagram 4-44

Versus an Odd Front Zone

Against odd front zones, it is a good idea to maintain a two-man front. This splits the front of the zone and often provides guards (1) and (2) with easy jump shots. When the ball is on a particular side, the two inside men, (4) and (5), may run an inside rotation. This happens when the ball is passed to (3) in the corner. (3) looks first to shoot, then tries to get the ball to the low post man

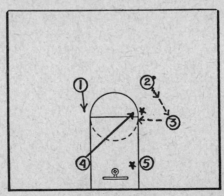

Diagram 4-45

on his side, (5). Then the offside post man (4) breaks to the ballside high post area. If the ball is passed to (4), (5) may be open in the low post area. See Diagram 4-45.

If (3) cannot get the ball to (4), (5) rolls away from the ball to the far low post area and (4) slides down. See Diagram 4-46.

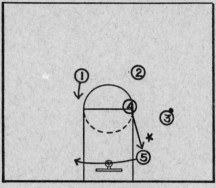

Diagram 4-46

If nothing develops, the ball is passed out to (2), who dribbles toward (1) and passes the ball to him. This gives (3) time to change corners. See Diagram 4-47.

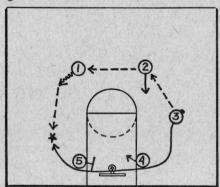

Diagram 4-47

As the ball changes sides, (5) and (4) screen the zone players and obstruct their path to cover (3).

Please note the moves of (2) and (1) in the first four diagrams. The offside guard (2) does not move to the point. He slides down a step or two and stays on his side of the court. The new onside guard (1) also must dribble toward (3) to get the ball to him, and when he wants to change sides, he dribbles toward the lane. These moves enable the offense to keep its two-man front, which puts much pressure on the odd front zone.

To provide motion and to force the zone to adjust, two front man moves may be used.

Guard Loop

The maneuver is used by the onside guard when he passes to (3). In Diagram 4-48, guard (1) passes to (3) and cuts quickly to the ballside high post area. If (3) can get the ball to him, he may shoot or pass to (4) or (5) inside the zone.

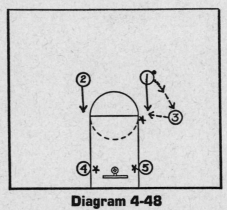

Diagram 4-48

If (1) is not open, (2) moves to the ballside and (1) loops to (2)'s former area. See Diagram 4-49.

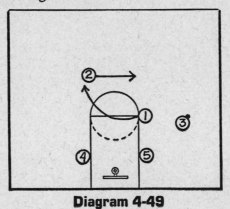

Diagram 4-49

Dribble Chase

The dribble chase is, in effect, another way to run a guard loop. As shown in Diagram 4-50, (1) dribbles at (2) and chases him. (2)

cuts to the free-throw line, where he may receive a pass if (3) gets
the ball from (1).

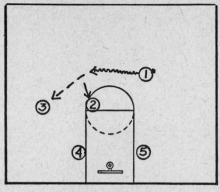

Diagram 4-50

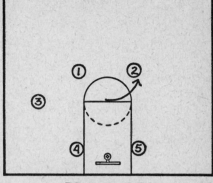

Diagram 4-51

If those passes are not forthcoming, (2) loops back to the
offside to maintain the two-man front. See Diagram 4-51.

Versus an Even Front Zone

Versus an even front zone, (1) takes the point and (2) moves to a
wing position. (3) then swings to (2)'s side to overload it. See
Diagram 4-52.

Diagram 4-52

From there, the team may run an inside rotation, a guard loop
(see Diagram 4-53), or a dribble chase (See Diagrams 4-54 and
4-55.). In addition, the team could change sides by having the point
man, (1), dribble to the unoccupied wing, and the offside guard (2)

will trail him to become the new point man. When this happens, (3) swings to the ballside corner. See Diagram 4-56.

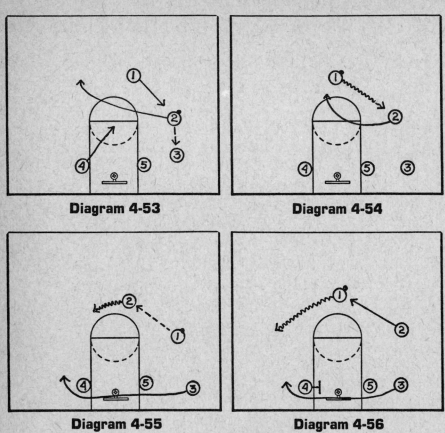

Diagram 4-53   **Diagram 4-54**

Diagram 4-55   **Diagram 4-56**

This zone offense gives the team the wherewithal to run against either even or odd front zones. The players are specialists and use primarily the same maneuvers against both types of zones. The two guards use the guard loop dribble chase and take the ball to the corner man (3). The two inside men, (4) and (5), post up during the overload and use an inside rotation. The baseline roamer, (3), fills the ballside corner. This offense overloads, overshifts, and tests the zone's corner and middle.

THE ZONE DEFENSE

5

This chapter is more or less an answer to chapter one. It is designed to provide counters to the zone offensive ideas that were suggested. As you study the zone, two facts will become very apparent. First, the zone defensive team members cannot afford to be off their guard at any time. They are called on to solve many problems and must be constantly aware of the position of the ball, as well as the position of the offensive players. Second, they cannot be lazy because they must move with each pass of the ball in order to execute their assignments. They also must be aware of, and prepared to meet, the following offensive team techniques and play situations.

STOPPING THE FAST BREAK

When a team plays zone defense, they can be sure that many teams plan to fastbreak them. The offense they run must be one that clearly designates who is responsible for defensive balance. Other ideas that may be used include the following.

Jamming the rebounder

A player or players may be assigned to attempt to stop the outlet pass by harassing the rebounder.

Stopping the outlet man

Some teams attempt to steal the outlet pass by anticipating the area into which it will be thrown. The person assigned to do this job, upon arriving late, may as a secondary goal attempt to make the outlet man pick up his dribble and pivot.

Retreating to the lane

This is a very important factor for zone teams attempting to stop a running team. All five defenders must retreat to the lane and then out to cover the ball in their area. This is another aspect of the basic rule that zone teams must play from the inside out.

Rapid transition

Some coaches simply say, "You are responsible for your area. If the opposition is scoring from there, your transition from offense to defense is too slow." This puts much pressure on the big man, who must cover the area nearest the basket, but simplifies individual responsibility.

FACING SPLITTING PERSONNEL ALIGNMENTS

When a zone team is split by the offensive alignment, the players have two options. They may adjust to the offense, or each player must be prepared to cover men in both marginal areas of his zone assignment. For example, the point man of a 1-3-1 zone may cover a splitting 2-1-2 offense by being part of a team clockwise rotation to a 2-1-2 zone, or by covering both of the front men as best he can. See X^1 in Diagram 5-1 and Diagram 5-2.

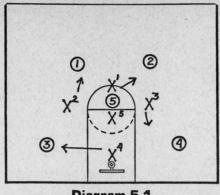
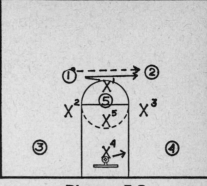

| Diagram 5-1 | Diagram 5-2 |

PREVENTING THE READING OF THE ZONE

To prevent the offense from reading the intent of the zone, the assignments may be varied or camouflaged. For example, a team that plans to play a zone that traps and pressures the perimeter passes may start out in a tight lane jamming zone and change on a key. The players could be instructed to give the opposition the outside shot until they get six points, and then switch to their basic plan.

PREPARING FOR STALLING TEAMS

The basketball rules state that when the defensive team is behind in the score, or the score is tied, they must force the action. The zone team must have a practiced plan that clearly tells them when they switch to man-to-man, or a method of converting to a one-half court pressure zone. This plan of when to pressure may vary with the opposition, but it is a necessity to save the precious seconds that often tick away. When in doubt, you may use the old rule that states "when the number of points you are behind is double the number of minutes on the clock, you must use pressure."

MINIMIZING OFFENSIVE REBOUNDS

Many zone teams are so conscious of the importance of rebounding that they sacrifice their fast break to strengthen their rebounding plan. All five defenders charge the boards when a shot is taken. The team fastbreaks only after a stolen pass. I personally feel that a team can send five men to the defensive boards and still make an outlet pass and fill the three lanes.

DENYING HIGH PERCENTAGE PERIMETER SHOTS

Most teams have some weak shooters and one or two high percentage shooters. The zone must get to the good shooters in a hurry. To do this, the defenders in that area must not make a deep drop when they are on the weak side. It also may be worthwhile to put a tall defender in the "good shooter" area.

DISRUPTING THE OFFENSIVE TEMPO

If the offensive team is moving the ball very well and controlling the game's tempo, you must disrupt their tempo. This can be done by playing the lanes, double teaming, or dropping way off them.

PLANNING TO STOP THE CROSSCOURT PASS

A coach must observe the type of crosscourt passes an opponent throws and work against them in practice. If this pass is very successful against the zone, a plan should be made to get to the passer more quickly and smother him so he cannot take the time to look crosscourt. The team's slides to cover the crosscourt pass must also be walked through in practice to avoid creating holes in the zone by double or no coverage.

COVERING CUTTERS

The zone team must tighten up when cutters go through. This should be little problem because each player has an assigned area slide and usually no definite player responsibility. Problems most often occur when the zone players attempt to rest instead of jamming the lane.

COVERING CHANGE OF PERIMETER ALIGNMENTS

These may be either even to odd, or odd to even. When they result in splitting situations, they should be treated as such. Either the zone must rotate (or make some other adjusting move), or a player may be required to hustle and cover everyone in his area.

Sometimes, if you are sure the opponent will change his offensive perimeter, you can have your defense fake one type of zone, but really be playing another. In Diagram 5-3 and Diagram 5-4, the apparent 2-3 zone is really a 1-2-2 zone in disguise, and once the cutter (2) goes through to change the offensive perimeter, the true 1-2-2 shape of the zone will be revealed.

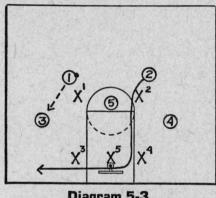
Diagram 5-3

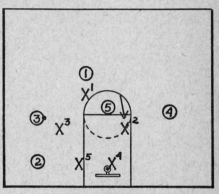
Diagram 5-4

TAKING ADVANTAGE OF THE OFFENSIVE OVERLOAD

Overloading a zone is not very functional. This is especially true if the offensive team does not maintain an offside rebounder. The team playing the zone must be careful not to get overextended to the ballside. They, too, must be careful to have offside rebounders when a shot is taken. The major problem arises for the defense when they must cover the corner. The first caution is not to cover too soon. You must wait until the ball is passed to a man in the corner and then approach him. The second is to make a compensating move when the offense has overloaded a side and is working to the corner. Two examples of compensating moves to handle this situation are the following.

A. The Flip Move

The flip move is used when the ball is passed from wing to corner. The man who covered the wing (X³ in Diagram 5-5) moves (flips) to the offside rebounding area as the ball is passed to the corner. X¹ would then cover the return pass to the wing area.

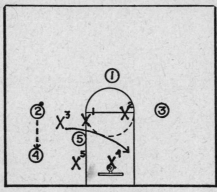

Diagram 5-5

B. The Check Move

This move is executed when the ball goes to the wing from the point. The defensive wing man on that side, X³, checks the man with the ball until the guard, X¹ gets there. X³ then releases to cover the corner. See Diagram 5-6 and Diagram 5-7.

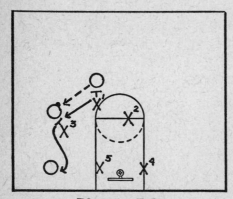
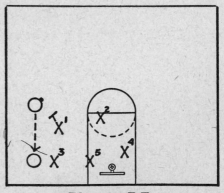

Diagram 5-6   **Diagram 5-7**

COUNTERING OVERSHIFTING OFFENSES

The only defensive answers to the offense's attempting to overshift them is having a willingness to move and having individuals with the ability to approach and retreat without getting off balance or out of position. This skill requires much practice time.

COVERING OVERSHIFTING PLUS SCREENS

When a zone player is screened, he has the same problems as does a man-to-man defender. The main difference is that the zone defender is sure he will have plenty of help. Because of this, he can gamble more and not worry as much about his direction of approach to the offensive man with the ball. This freedom should make his job much easier.

PREPARING FOR OFFENSES THAT WILL TEST THE CORNER

Seldom will you be beaten from the corner. It is one of the toughest positions on the court from which to shoot. The defensive players should be aware of the shooting capability of the man in their corner, cover it only after a pass is made to that area, and should be taught to approach quickly without sacrificing balance.

PREPARING FOR OFFENSES THAT WILL TEST THE MIDDLE

Zones must work very hard on keeping the ball out of the middle. When it gets to the middle, they must be sure who comes up to cover and who jams the two lay-up areas.

COVERING OFFENSES THAT WILL GO SECOND SIDE

A zone team must also work hard to be able to cover the second side without getting out of position or sacrificing defensive capability. If it appears the offense is attempting to move the ball just to move the defense, and with little thought of shooting, either of two extreme defensive plays will help. The zone may drop off and jam the lane, or spread out and attempt to deter or even intercept the perimeter pass.

MATCHING UP WITH OFFENSES THAT TAKE ADVANTAGE OF YOUR PERSONNEL

If you notice the offense is taking advantage of personnel match-ups, tell your defenders to first match-up with a certain man, and then play zone from there.

ZONING TEAMS THAT ATTEMPT TO RUN THEIR MAN-TO-MAN OR MOVING OFFENSE

A team playing a matching zone or one that puts pressure on the perimeter and attempts to intercept passes may be hurt by moving offenses. It is wise when this occurs to retreat to a rigid, jam-the-middle type defense. The opposite is true if the offense is standing still. This is an opportunity to match-up or a time to take chances and attempt to anticipate and intercept.

HANDLING THE DRIBBLER

Perimeter Dribble

The key to handling a perimeter dribble is defensive talk. The defender into whose area the dribbler enters must release the original defender by saying, "I have him" or "Mine." He may even use his hands to push his teammate back to his assigned area.

Penetration Dribble

The defenders must again be reminded that the zone is played from the inside out. The key defensive slides of a zone player area approach and retreat. He must be coached to execute them properly and informed that in most cases it is better to give up the outside shot than permit a dribbler to get to the heart of the zone.

PREPARING FOR TEAMS WHOSE PLAYERS RECEIVE THE BALL IN AN ALL-PURPOSE POSITION

In sports, the actor usually beats the reactor. The player who must zone the area in which a well-prepared player is located must act. He must vary his approaches by, at different times, playing off him, forcing him to dribble, playing in the lane between him and the ball, and approaching him from different directions. If your play becomes stereotyped, you will become the reactor, thus diminishing your chance of success.

ADJUSTING TO TEAMS THAT PLAY A TALL PLAYER OUT FRONT

This is just another example of compensating for bad personnel match-ups. If a tall offensive man is playing out front and shooting or passing over your smaller defenders, you should first have him picked up high to see if he can dribble. If this doesn't work, you must rearrange your personnel.

TEAMS THAT SLIDE INTO THE ZONES' WEAK AREAS

This is another splitting move and must be covered by some sort of an adjustment, such as a rotation. If not, each defender must cover all defenders in his area to the best of his ability.

POST-TO-POST PASSES

High Post to Low Post Passes

To help prevent this pass, the original picture given by a zone must be a tight one. All five defenders should start with one foot in the lane. They must have their arms up and move out to the ball. Once the ball is passed to the side, the front man or men, depending on the type of zone, must protect the high post area.

When the ball has been passed successfully to the high post area, the zone must again collapse. All five defenders must get in the lane and get their hands up. Diagram 5-8 shows a 2-3 zone collapsing after a pass to the high post area.

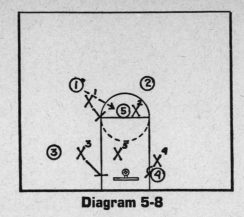

Diagram 5-8

Note how X^3 and X^4 collapse to protect the vital low post area.

The same is true from a one-man front zone. Diagram 5-9 shows a pass to the high post versus a 1-2-2 zone. Note how X^4 and X^3 collapse to protect the low post area.

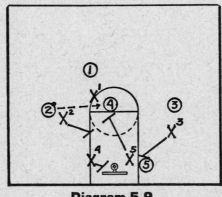

Diagram 5-9

Low Post Passing to High Post Cutting Down

If this appears to be one of your opponent's key zone offensive plans, you must deny the pass to the low post man. This may entail your big men playing strong to the ballside. To compensate, the offside zone players must sag a little deeper. Diagram 5-10 shows X^4, the lead big man of a 1-2-2 zone, denying a pass from the wing to the low post area. Note X^5 and X^3 slides.

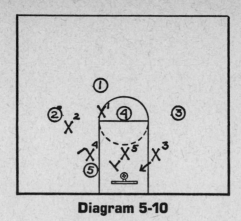

Diagram 5-10

In Diagram 5-11, X^5, the middle big man of a 2-3 zone, makes the overplay, and the offside back man, X^4, plus offside front man, X^2, must make the deep sag.

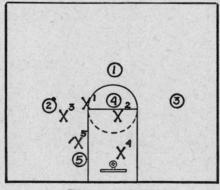

Diagram 5-11

Once the pass is made to the low post man, the zone players must jam the lane. The onside point man, X^1, may be given the job of cutting down with the offensive high post man, (4), to deny the pass to him. See Diagram 5-12.

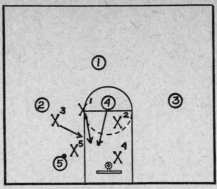

Diagram 5-12

This will weaken the defense on the perimeter, but deny the high post man (4) a lay-up or short jump shot.

ANTICIPATING THE PRESSURE DEFENSE

Zone teams must be prepared to face more pressure defenses. Many coaches, fearing they will have trouble with their offense against the zone team, try to win on defense with some sort of pressure.

HAVING FAITH IN YOUR ZONE DEFENSE

Much of the talk about liking to play against zones is like whistling in the dark. Most teams spend more time on their man-to-man offense; there are more man-to-man offenses available; teams usually face more man-to-man defenses; and if a zone is played well, you have to hit from the outside. Once your zone gains respect among the people in your league, it doesn't take too many wins to turn this feeling to fear. Once you attain that, it is a big step toward the league championship.

Along with these many ideas about zone defense, a team should spend much practice time discussing the two basic types of offensive components they will face.

AN INSIDE ROTATION

An inside rotation occurs when there is a movement in the ballside high and low post areas. The posts are vacated, and then cuts are made into the area. Diagram 5-13 shows a type of inside rotation. The ball is passed to (2) at the wing. He looks to both ballside post areas. If he does not pass inside, the low post man (5) swings across the lane, the high post man (4) drops down, and the offside wing man (3) fills the high post area.

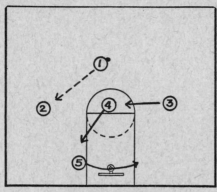

Diagram 5-13

The defenders must ignore the movement and complete their assignments. For example, using a 1-2-2 zone, the point man, X^1, must shut down the high post area. The ballside big man must deny (5) until he vacates and then step into (4)'s cut as he comes down. See Diagram 5-14 and Diagram 5-15.

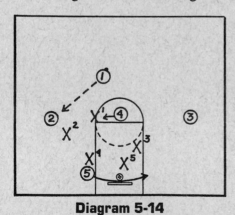

Diagram 5-14

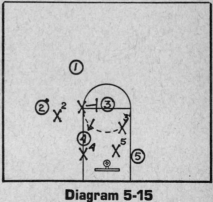

Diagram 5-15

A PERIMETER ROTATION

Probably the most often used zone play is the perimeter rotation. This happens, as shown in Diagram 5-16, when wing man

(2) passes to (4) in the corner and cuts through to the offside wing; the perimeter then rotates toward the ball. This is done by the point man (1) replacing (2), and the offside wing man (3) takes the point.

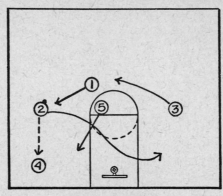

Diagram 5-16

As shown in Diagram 5-16, this is usually accompanied by a high post (5) to low post move.

The perimeter zone players must be taught to look for the release man. Whenever a man in your zone passes and cuts through, someone will usually replace him. He is the release man and will probably be your next man to cover.

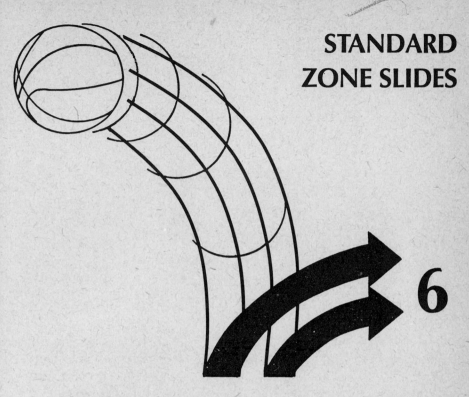

STANDARD ZONE SLIDES

6

One of the best ways to teach the zone defense is to show the similarities of odd and even front zones. Once the players understand that the slides of a 1-2-2 zone are much like those of a 2-3 zone, they have little trouble playing either zone.

THE 1-2-2 ZONE

The importance of the initial spacing of any zone cannot be overstressed. For a 1-2-2- zone, the spacing is as follows.

Front

X¹—Point Man

The point man should start one step above the head of the key. From there, he is seldom wrong if he will stay between the ball and an imaginary dot at the center of the free-throw line.

X^2, X^3—Wing Men

The wing men should start as high as the free-throw line extended and one step outside the lane.

X^4, X^5—Deep Men

The two deep men should stay eight feet apart at all times. Initially, they are both in the lane and outside the front vertical plane of the rim. See Diagram 6-1.

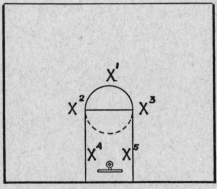

Diagram 6-1

Side

When the ball is passed to a side, as to X^2's side in Diagram 6-2, X^2 takes the man with the ball, X^1 stays between the ball and an imaginary dot in the center of the free-throw line, and X^4 moves toward the ballside corner. How far out X^4 will move will depend on whether the corner is occupied by an offensive player. X^5 stays eight feet from X^4. The rule for the offside wing man, X^3, is to stay between the ball and the offside corner.

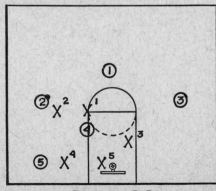

Diagram 6-2

Corner

When the ball goes to the corner, three different types of slides are possible.

A. Triangle Slide

When the offense is very strong inside, triangle slides may be used. This involves X^2 dropping between X^4 and X^5 to form a triangle. X^2 will be at the apex of the triangle and ten feet from the baseline. This slide jams the middle and makes it very difficult to get the ball inside. See Diagram 6-3.

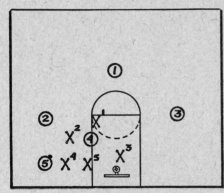
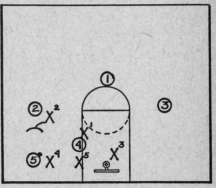

Diagram 6-3   **Diagram 6-4**

B. Lane Slide

When the offense moves the ball well and has good perimeter shooters, the lane slide may be used. X^2 again is the determining player. This time he moves between the wing man and the corner man with the ball and jams the perimeter passing lane. See Diagram 6-4.

C. Trap Slide

If the offense is composed of players who are not efficient ball handlers, the trap slide may be used. This time as the ball is passed from wing to corner, X^2 calls "Trap!" and follows the ball to the corner to form a double team with X^4. This tells X^1 he must cover the wing man, and X^3 that he must cover the point. X^5 is the safety man and must stay between the ball and the basket. It helps if he keeps his shoulders parallel with the backboard. See Diagram 6-5 and Diagram 6-6.

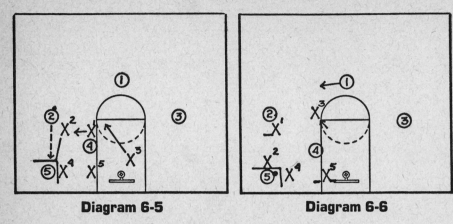

Diagram 6-5   **Diagram 6-6**

As soon as the ball is out of the trap, X^5 must call out "Zone," and the five defenders should hustle to assume their basic positions.

Pass to Post

When the ball is passed to the post, the offisde deep man (X^5 in Diagram 6-7), must cover it and the onside deep man, X^4, must get between him and the basket. The two wing men, X^2 and X^3, must pinch in to their respective lay-up slots. X^1 again stays between the ball and an imaginary dot in the center of the free-throw lane.

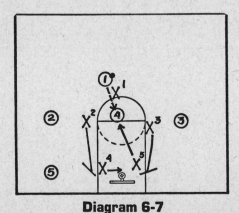

Diagram 6-7

Pass Out of Post

When the ball is passed out of the post, the back deep man, X^4 (who is closest to the basket), slides to the side and the front deep man, who is covering the post man, drops toward the basket. In effect, the pass to the post coverted the 1-2-2 zone to a 1-3-1, and the pass out returned it to a 1-2-2 shape. See Diagram 6-8.

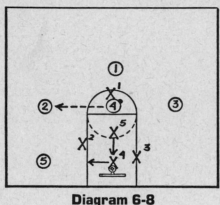

Diagram 6-8

THE 2-3 ZONE

Once the players have learned the 1-2-2 slides, the next step is to relate them to the 2-3 slides.

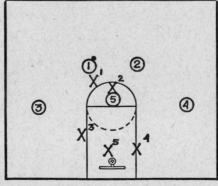

Diagram 6-9

Front

As shown in Diagram 6-9, the 2-3 zone is composed of: an onside front man, X^1; an offside front man, X^2; a middle man, X^5;

and two wing men, X^3 and X^4. For the initial picture, the offside front man, X^2, covers the high post, and both wing man, X^3 and X^4 should start in the lane. All five defenders should have their hands up and make the lane appear to be crowded.

Side

From here, the 2-3 slides are the same as those of a 1-2-2 if the coach can teach the players the following points:

- The slides of the onside front man, X^1, of a 2-3 zone are the same as those of a point man of a 1-2-2 zone.
- The slides of the offside front man, X^2, are the same as those of an offside wing man of a 1-2-2 zone.
- The slides of the onside wing man, X^3, of a 2-3 zone are the same as those of an onside wing man of a 1-2-2 zone.
- The slides of the middle man, X^5, of a 2-3 zone are the same as those of a lead back man of a 1-2-2 zone.
- The slides of the offside wing man, X^4, of a 2-3 zone are the same as those of a trailing back man of a 1-2-2 zone.

Observing these rules as the ball goes to the side, the players should make the following moves:

- X^1, the onside front man of the 2-3 zone, stays between the ball and an imaginary dot in the center of the free-throw line (as per the point man, X^1, of the 1-2-2 zone).
- X^2, the offside front man of the 2-3 zone, stays between the ball and the offside corner (as per the offside wing man, X^3, of the 1-2-2 zone).
- X^3, the onside wing man of the 2-3 zone, covers the ball (as per the onside wing man, X^2, of the 1-2-2 zone).
- X^4, the offside wing man of the 2-3 zone, trails X^5 by eight feet toward the ballside corner (as would the trailing back man, X^5, of a 1-2-2 zone).
- X^5, the middle man of the 2-3 zone, prepares to cover the corner (as would the lead back man, X^4, of a 1-2-2 zone). See Diagrams 6-10 and 6-11.

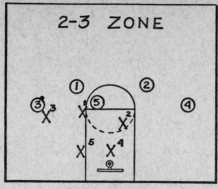

Diagram 6-10

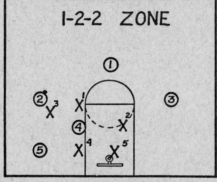

Diagram 6-11

Corner

When the ball is passed to the corner, the following moves should be taken:

- X^1, the onside front man of the 2-3 zone, stays between the ball and an imaginary dot in the center of the free-throw line (as per the point man, X^1, of the 1-2-2 zone).
- X^2, the offside front man of the 2-3 zone, stays between the ball and the offside corner (as per the offside wing man, X^3, of the 1-2-2 zone).
- X^3, the onside wing man of the 2-3 zone, may use a triangle, lane, or trap slide, depending on the situation (as per the onside wing man, X^2, of a 1-2-2 zone).

- X[4], the offside wing man of the 2-3 zone, stays eight feet behind X[5] as he moves toward the corner (as per the trailing back man, X[5], of the 1-2-2 zone).

- X[5], the middle man of the 2-3 zone, covers the ball in the corner (as per the leading big man, X[4], of the 1-2-2 zone). See Diagrams 6-12 and 6-13.

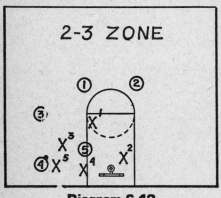

Diagram 6-12

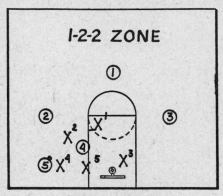

Diagram 6-13

Once these perimeter slides have been mastered and the team is aware that they should play a 2-3 zone against an even perimeter and a 1-2-2 against an odd front perimeter, the next step is rotation. They must be taught to make the initial front match-up by, when necessary, rotating from an odd front zone (1-2-2) to an even-fronted one (2-3). This is done by having the quarterback, X[1], call out "2" or "Even" and each zone player rotating clockwise to cover the first man in that area. See Diagrams 6-14 and 6-15.

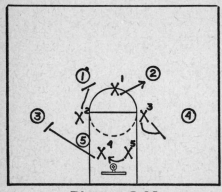

Diagram 6-14

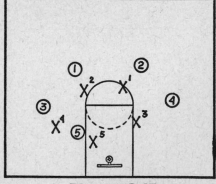

Diagram 6-15

This converts the 1-2-2 zone to a 2-3 zone and matches the even fronted perimeter.

When it is necessary to convert from an even front zone (2-3) to an odd front (1-2-2), the quarterback calls "1" or "Odd," and each zone player rotates counter-clockwise to cover the first man in that area. See Diagrams 6-16 and 6-17.

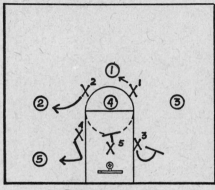

Diagram 6-16

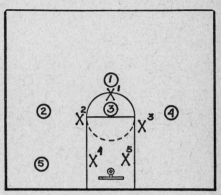

Diagram 6-17

The team is now prepared to play either a 2-3 or 1-2-2 zone, and has the wherewithal to change from one to the other. From there, it is a matter of teaching both the quarterback to recognize the perimeter, and call it out, and the other players to make the proper reaction.

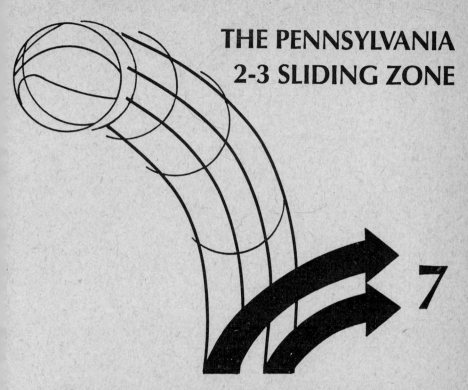

THE PENNSYLVANIA 2-3 SLIDING ZONE

7

One of the zones we used at Eastern Montana College was the Pennsylvania 2-3 Sliding Zone originated by John Egli. It provided a viable method of covering both odd and even front offenses.

The ideal personnel for this zone would be three inside men with fairly equal rebounding ability and two very quick outside men.

The following adaptation of this zone is described in the vocabulary that we developed while using it.

VERSUS EVEN FRONT OFFENSIVE PERIMETERS

The easiest perimeter for a 2-3 zone to cover is, of course, an even-fronted one.

Front

When the ball is out front, as shown in Diagram 7-1, the onside front man, X^1, plays up on the ball; the offside front man, X^2, is responsible for jamming the high post area, and if there is an offensive player in the high post area, he should touch him; the middle of the back three men, X^5, is three to five feet in front of the basket; and the two wing men, X^3 and X^4, start each with one foot in the lane. We make a big point of playing zone from the inside out. This provides benefits that are both physical and psychological. All five defenders are instructed to assume a wide defensive stance. The sum total of this is that the lane appears to be completely jammed.

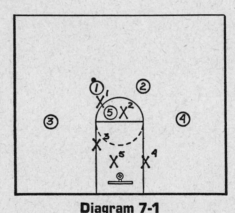

Diagram 7-1

Side

When the ball is passed to the side, the wing man on that side, X^3, comes up to cover; the onside front man, X^1, jams the high post area; the offside front man, X^2, jams the middle of the lane. The slides of X^5 and X^4 will be determined by the circumstances. If there is a man on the corner, X^5 must slide at least out of the lane to be prepared to cover him, and X^4 will stay eight feet behind X^5. See Diagram 7-2.

If there is no one in the corner, X^5 stays in the lane area, with X^4 eight feet behind him. See Diagram 7-3.

If there is a post man and no one in the corner, X^5 must front him. See Diagram 7-4.

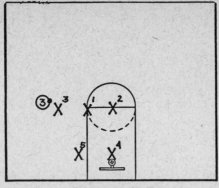

Diagram 7-2

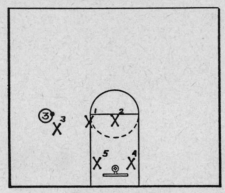

Diagram 7-3

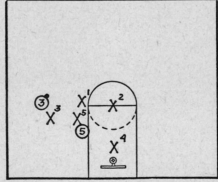

Diagram 7-4

Pass to the Corner

When the ball is passed to the corner, X^5 must cover it. X^1 jams the three-quarter post area, X^2 slides inside the free-throw line, and

X^4 is eight feet behind X^5, or behind a post man, if there is one. The key man is the wing man who was covering the ball at the side position. He can make one of two slides.

He may make the move we call "flip," shown in Diagram 7-5. This consists of hustling to the offside lay-up area.

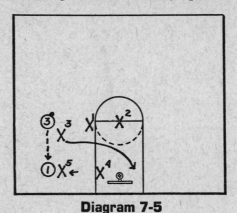

Diagram 7-5

He may use the slide we call "post," shown in Diagram 7-6. This consists of sliding in between X^5 and X^4 and fronting the post, if there is one.

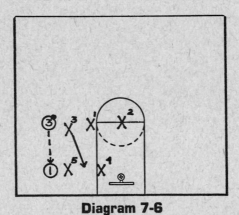

Diagram 7-6

Either of these slides results in a realignment of the three back men. This is the reason this zone works best with back men of equal size and/or equal rebounding ability.

Pass from Corner Back to Wing

This is the slide that demands quickness from the two front men (X^1 and X^2). As the ball is passed back to the offensive wing man, X^1 (the onside front man) must cover two passes coming out of the corner. So he hustles out and covers the wing man and then takes the next pass out front. To facilitate X^1's covering two passes, the offside front man, X^2, must protect by being prepared to pick up anyone who drives by X^1. See Diagrams 7-7 and 7-8.

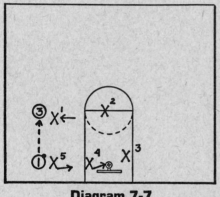

Diagram 7-7

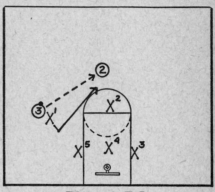

Diagram 7-8

From there, the same front, side, to corner, and out of corner slides could be repeated.

Pass to Post

Anytime the ball is passed to the post area inside the free-throw line, the middle back man, X^5, covers and the two wing men, X^3 and X^4, must pinch in to their respective lay-up slots. See Diagram 7-9.

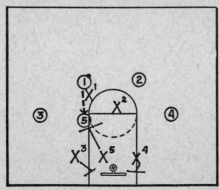

Diagram 7-9

Corner Strategy

A team may predetermine to use either the "post" or "flip" slides. They also can use them both at once by utilizing the "post" slide except when the wing man cuts through. They would then use the "flip" slides. This often frustrates the offense and has the appearance that this zone goes through with cutters.

Diagram 7-10 shows a pass to the corner when the wing man (2) does not cut through.

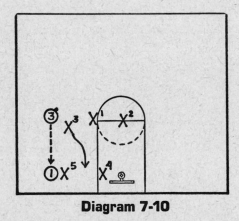

Diagram 7-10

Diagram 7-11 shows a pass to the corner and a subsequent cut by the offensive wing man (2).

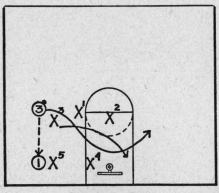

Diagram 7-11

VERSUS ODD FRONT OFFENSIVE PERIMETERS

Front

When the offense uses an odd perimeter, an immediate adjustment must be made by the two defensive front men, X^1 and X^2. X^1 must cover the wing man on his side and X^2 must take the lone point man. See Diagram 7-12.

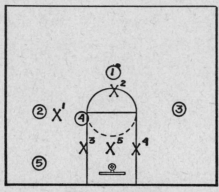

Diagram 7-12

This tilting of the front men results in what we call an "easy" side and a "flip" (or post) side.

A. "Easy" Side

Front to Easy Side

When the ball is passed from the point to the wing covered by X^1, we call this the "easy side." That is to say, the coverage on that side is easy. X^1 covers the wing man and this frees X^3 to cover the corner without disturbing the three in a line arrangement of the back men. See Diagram 7-13.

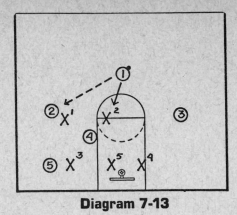

Diagram 7-13

To Easy Corner

When the ball is passed to the corner, X^3 takes it and X^1 can jam inside or bother the return pass. This would, of course, depend on the strengths and weaknesses of the opposition. See Diagram 7-14.

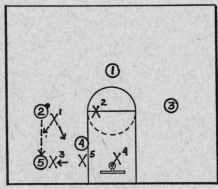

Diagram 7-14

Out of Easy Corner

X^1 does not have to cover two passes out of the corner. When the pass goes from his wing to the point, he jams the high post area as per the assignment of the offside front man.

B. "Flip" Side

All that happens on the flip side is the normal 2-3 slides.

Front

X² takes the point man, X¹ jams the lane, X⁴ is prepared to cover the wing, X⁵ checks the corner, and X³ stays eight feet behind X⁵. See Diagram 7-15.

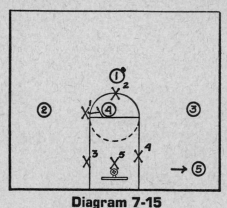

Diagram 7-15

Side

When the ball is passed to the side, X⁴ covers it; X⁵ prepares to (a) cover the corner, (b) jam the lane, or (c) front the post (depending on the situation); X³ is still eight feet behind X⁵; and X¹ and X² jam the high post area. See Diagram 7-16.

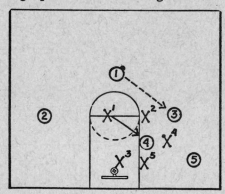

Diagram 7-16

Pass to Corner

When the ball is passed to the corner, X⁵ takes it, X³ stays eight feet behind him, X⁴ flips (or posts), and X¹ and X² continue to jam the high post area. See Diagram 7-17.

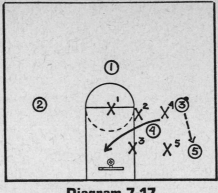

Diagram 7-17

Pass Out of Corner

Since this is the flip side, X^2 must take two passes coming out of the corner. See Diagram 7-18 and Diagram 7-19.

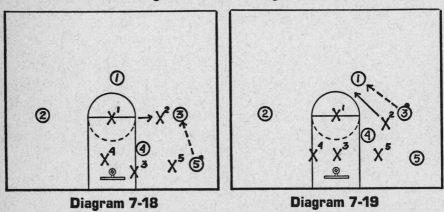

Diagram 7-18   **Diagram 7-19**

From there, the same slides may be repeated on either side.

The coverage of the post is the same as when facing an even perimeter.

This zone keeps the big men close to the basket, covers either an even or odd front perimeter effectively, allows a team without a big man to rebound well, and is easy to learn.

ZONE CHECKER DRILLS

When teaching the Pennsylvania Zone, as with any other zone, I would use the Zone Checker Drills. These drills are basic to playing a zone defense. They are teaching devices, that are good for conditioning and that build confidence by convincing the players that through teamwork they can thoroughly cover the zone's vital areas.

Five players are placed on defense against an offensive team with men located in each of the potential zone offensive areas. This may be more than five players. The offense then moves the ball at a reasonable tempo, and the five defenders must cover them.

The drills should follow a definite progression and involve the defense's covering the following points.

A. An Even Perimeter with No Post Man. See Diagram 7-20.

B. An Odd Perimeter with No Post Man. See Diagram 7-21.

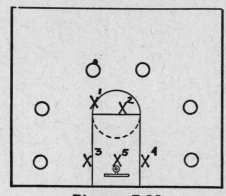
Diagram 7-20

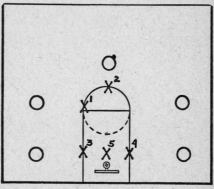
Diagram 7-21

These two exercises are simply to practice the perimeter coverage versus the two basic zone offensive alignments.

An optional drill that may be run at this point is a recognition drill. This is done by having five offensive players come up court several times and vary their offensive alignment, between an even and odd front. This drill is run primarily for the guards, who must quickly recognize the shape of the offensive perimeter. At the start of the season, it might be wise to have them call out "Odd" or "Even," depending on the offense.

C. Even Perimeter Plus a High and Low Post. See Diagram 7-22.

D. An Odd Perimeter Plus a High and Low Post. See Diagram 7-23.

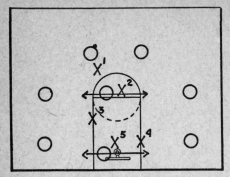
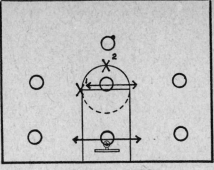

Diagram 7-22   **Diagram 7-23**

These two exercises combine perimeter coverage with the problems of keeping the ball out of the post positions and covering up when it does enter either post. We work particularly hard preventing post-to-post passes.

E. Changing Perimeter with No Post Men. See Diagrams 7-24, 7-25, and 7-26.

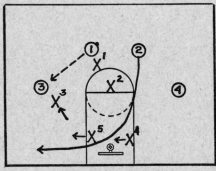

Diagram 7-24

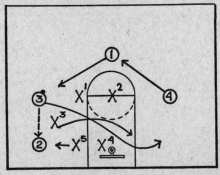

Diagram 7-25

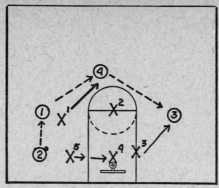

Diagram 7-26

F. Changing Perimeter with Post Men. See Diagrams 7-27, 7-28, 7-29, 7-30, and 7-31.

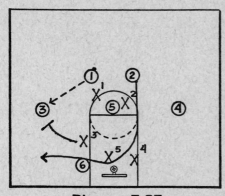

Diagram 7-27

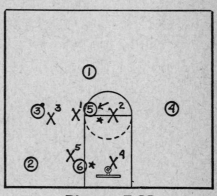

Diagram 7-28

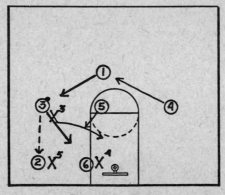

Diagram 7-29

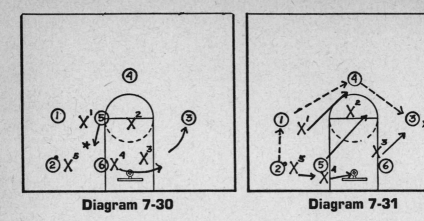

Diagram 7-30   **Diagram 7-31**

When used every day in practice, these drills make the zone slides automatic. They are based on the most common zone alignments and movements. In the event a team has an opponent with a unique or problem-causing alignment or movement, its components should be included in a similar drill.

THE MONSTER-MAN ZONE

8

In writing about the zone defense, I would be remiss if I did not include the Monster-Man Zone. We originated this zone at Eastern Montana College. Its development was due primarily to the fact that zone teams must be prepared to match odd, even, and changing perimeters. The key word for modern zone coaches is adjustment. The Monster-Man Zone allows a team to make all these necessary adjustments with just one man (the Monster Man).

The Monster Man's rules are simple. If the offense has a two-man front, he covers the front man on the right. If the offense has a one-man or odd front, he drops back and covers both corners. He becomes the baseline chaser of a 1-3-1 zone. See Diagrams 8-1 and 8-2.

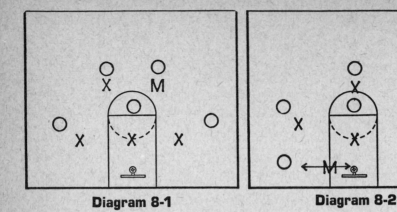

Diagram 8-1   **Diagram 8-2**

The other four men follow their rules and make the same slides, regardless of the shape of the offense perimeter.

Wing Men

The wing men, X^2 and X^3, have these rules.

BALLSIDE: If there is an open man on your side and the ball goes to him, you must come up and take him. (If X^1 and the Monster are following their rules correctly, the wing man will usually cover a side or corner man.)

OFFSIDE: When the ball goes opposite, you stay eight feet from our defensive post man, X^4.

PIVOT: When the ball goes into the pivot, you must run for the basket.

Point Man

Our point man, X^1, has these rules.

- If they have a two-man front, take the man on the left and the Monster will take the other.
- If they have an odd-man front, take the offensive point man.

His sagging rules are to stay between the ball and an imaginary dot in the center of the free-throw line when the ball comes his way.

When it goes toward the Monster, he must stay between the ball and the offside corner.

Defensive Post Man

Our defensive post man must guard the offensive pivot man, protect the basket, and cover the corner if the Monster does not.

To learn to apply these rules, we use the following drills.

Drill 1—Odd-Man Front (No Monster)

We set up a six-man zone offense composed of an odd perimeter with two corner men, a point man, two side men, and a post man, as shown in Diagram 8-3.

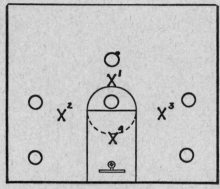

Diagram 8-3

We then cover this exaggerated situation with only four men. This drill is our confidence builder. When the players find they can cover six offensive men with four defenders, it is easy to tell them that we will be very tough five-on-five. Diagrams 8-4, 8-5, 8-6, 8-7, and 8-8 show the defensive slides for this drill.

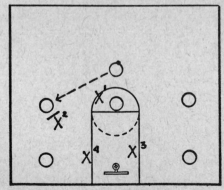

Diagram 8-4

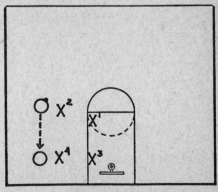

Diagram 8-5

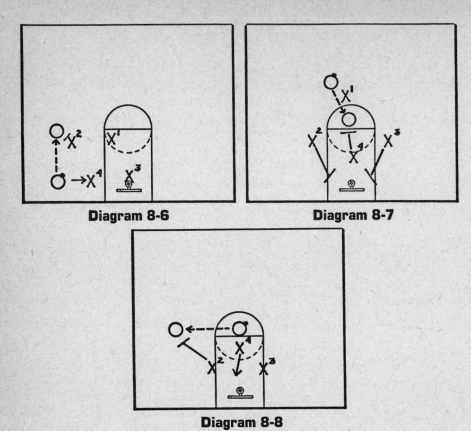

Diagram 8-6   Diagram 8-7

Diagram 8-8

This drill also teaches the offside wing that he must stay eight feet from X^4 or the offensive pivot man is open; X^1 that he should sag deep enough; and all defenders that this zone defense requires hustle.

Drill 2—Odd-Man Front (with Monster)

We then add the Monster. This makes X^4's job very easy. The same slides are used except the Monster now covers both corners. This allows X^4 to concentrate on rebounding.

Drill 3—Even-Man Front (with Monster)

The Monster is needed to cover one of the front men. In this drill, an exaggerated situation is used again. The offense has seven men: two front men, two side men, two corner men, and a pivot man. Practically the same slides are used as in Drill 1. See Diagrams 8-9, 8-10, 8-11, 8-12, and 8-13.

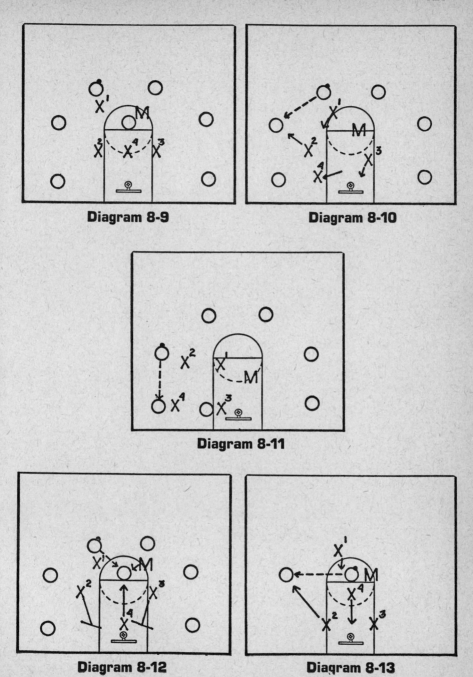

Diagram 8-9

Diagram 8-10

Diagram 8-11

Diagram 8-12

Diagram 8-13

This, again, is a great confidence builder because five defenders are covering seven.

Drill 4—Even to Odd 5-on-5 (with Monster)

In this drill, we face what we refer to as the standard zone offense. We have found that 50 percent of the teams we see play use part or all of this zone-offense sequence.

Two offensive men bring the ball upcourt. This tells the Monster it is a two-man front and he must play up front. One guard passes to his side man and a guard cuts through to the corner. This changes their perimeter front even to odd and tells the Monster he must go through the cutting guard and then cover both corners. See Diagrams 8-14 and 8-15.

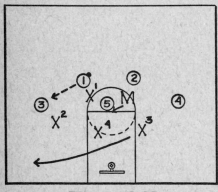

Diagram 8-14

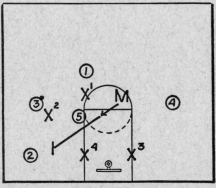

Diagram 8-15

From here the standard offense is for the side man to pass to the corner and cut through. The offense then attempts to reverse the ball to the cutter. See Diagrams 8-16 and 8-17 for this offensive play and our defensive counters.

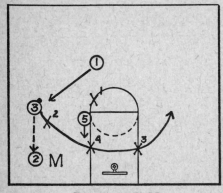

Diagram 8-16

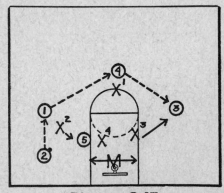

Diagram 8-17

This play teaches the Monster to convert from even to odd and to hustle to cover both corners.

Some coaching points we stress when teaching the Monster Zone are as follows:

- Two men usually bring the ball upcourt. We can create midcourt pressure and retreat to the Monster Zone.
- We must always play from the inside out. We do not want to get hurt inside.
- Most zone offenses are stereotyped, mechanical, and not often functional.
- The Monster is usually a small man and never plays behind post men.
- Zone offenses often use a big man in the corner. It is wise for the Monster to block him out when a shot is taken.
- Our point men must not try to help the side men versus odd fronts. Many baskets are scored from his area.
- Versus a two-man front, the offside defensive guard must jam the high post area.
- When the Monster cannot cover the corner, and our big men must, the front defenders should make a deep sag.
- If you are guarding the man with the ball, stay with him until he gets rid of it.

The Monster Zone allows us to cover odd, even, and changing perimeters. The adjustments are made by one man (the Monster) and often confuse the offense into thinking we are playing man-to-man. The net result of the use of these rules and drills is a hustling, confident team defense.

THE MONSTER-MAN-PLUS-ONE ZONE DEFENSE

At least once during every season, a coach is faced with the problem of defensing the big, tough pivot man. In many cases, a straight man-to-man match-up is out of the question.

> NOTE: The two standard pivot-man stoppers are the box-and-one and the diamond-and-one. They are both gambles because each of them is based on an assumption of where the other four offensive men will be stationed.

The following Monster-Man-Plus-One Defense adjusts with the offense, and still allows man-to-man coverage on the big man (5). The four-man zone always starts in a box formation and has the following rules.

X^1 and X^2

Rather than have a designated Monster Man, this defense may utilize either front man as the Monster.

The two front men in the box meet the offensive guards at midcourt and create pressure. After that they are told if your guard stays out front, stay with him. If he goes through, call out "Cutter" and follow him to the baseline, then drop off and cover the ballside corner, as would the back chaser on a 1-3-1 zone. (See X^2 of Diagram 8-18. In this Diagram X^2 went through and, in effect, became the Monster Man.) If the other front man of your zone calls "Cutter" first, you must remain out front.

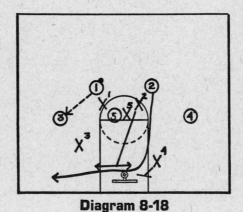

Diagram 8-18

X^3 and X^4

When the ball is on your side, you cover the man at the free-throw line extended (see X^4 of Diagram 8-19). If no one is there, take the man in the corner. Don't cover them unless they have the ball or are about to get it. When the ball goes to the opposite side of the court, jam in on the pivot man (see X^3 of Diagram 8-19).

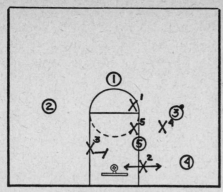

Diagram 8-19

NOTE: His man-to-man defender, X^5, will be in front of him and you must help on the lob pass. Play it as if it is being thrown to you. When the ball goes into the pivot, both wings must run for the basket.

Jamming the Pivot Area

To further congest the free-throw lane area, the guards are given these instructions: if both offensive guards stay out front, the offside defensive guard must jam the high post area. See X^2 of Diagram 8-20.

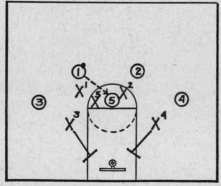

Diagram 8-20

NOTE: It may seem like a lot to expect your defensive guards to create pressure at mid-court and also jame the middle on the offside, but the pressure is a hit and retreat type, and any guard must be very mobile to be effective.

If a defensive guard has gone through with his man, he should be able to cover the ballside corner and also help when the ball goes into the post area. See X^2 of Diagram 8-21.

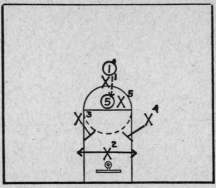

Diagram 8-21

Man-to-Man Defender X^5

The man guarding the big pivot man (X^5) is assigned to front the big man (5) anywhere inside the free-throw line. In order to front him this high, we must have plenty of help under the basket. This is why our wing men are told to play their defense from the inside out and go for the basket when the ball goes into the pivot.

> NOTE: We call this the pivot pinch and devote much time to practicing it.

The man-to-man defender should contest every cut made by the big man. When a shot is taken, he must definitely block him away from the boards.

> BENEFITS: This defense has the same feature of the box-and-one and diamond-and-one defenses in that it congests the pivot area and provides man-to-man coverage on the big pivot man. It has the added advantage of matching the zone offensive perimeter on practically a man-to-man basis.

THE MONSTER-MAN-PLUS-ONE ZONE USING THE PENNSYLVANIA SLIDING ZONE

The Monster-Man-Plus-One Zone concept can also be adapted to Coach John Egli's Pennsylvania Sliding Zone.

Even-Man Front

Against a two-man front, both defensive guards, X^1 and X^2, stay out front and the following slides are used. See Diagram 8-22.

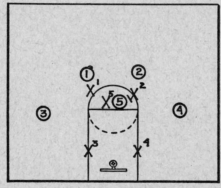

Diagram 8-22

Front

In Diagram 8-22, X^5 is playing (5), the strong offensive player, man-to-man, and the other four have matched the offensive perimeter.

Front to Side

When the ball goes to the side, X^4 comes up and covers it, X^2 and X^1 jam the high post area, X^3 slides across the lane, and X^5 continues to guard (5) man-to-man. See Diagram 8-23.

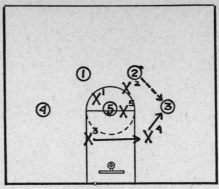

Diagram 8-23

Side to Corner

When the ball goes to the corner, X^3 covers it and X^4 goes over the top to X^3's side, X^1 and X^2 jam, and X^5 guards (5) as he comes to the ballside low post area. See Diagram 8-24. In the event (5) did not come to the ball, X^4 would slide into the ballside low post area. See Diagram 8-25.

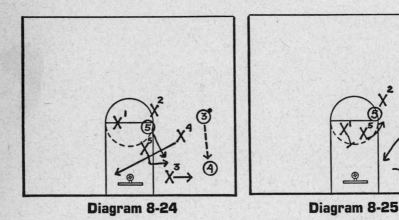

Diagram 8-24   **Diagram 8-25**

Corner Back to Side

From here, the front man on the ballside must take the next two passes coming out of the corner. Thus, as the ball goes from corner to side, X^2 covers this pass, X^3 loosens up, X^1 jams from the offside, and X^4 is now the offside wing man. See Diagram 8-26.

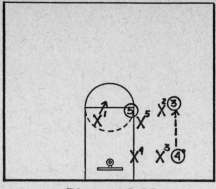

Diagram 8-26

Side Back to Front

When the ball goes out front, X^2 takes this second pass out of the corner and the zone is back in its original shape. The only change is that X^3 and X^4 have switched sides. See Diagram 8-27.

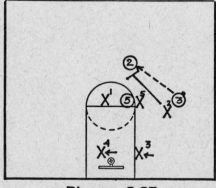

Diagram 8-27

Odd-Man Front

This means the offense is in a one-man front, so guard X^1 releases and will cover both corners.

Front

X^2 takes the point and X^1 is now prepared to cover both corners. See Diagram 8-28.

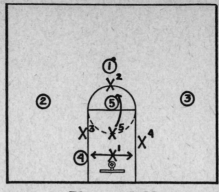

Diagram 8-28

Front to Side

X⁴ takes the pass to the side, X² jams the high post, X¹ is prepared to cover the ballside corner, X³ jams to the offside rebounding area, and X⁵ plays (5) in a forcing, overplaying man-to-man. See Diagram 8-29.

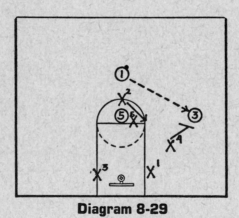

Diagram 8-29

Side to Corner

When the ball goes from side to corner, X¹ covers the corner, X³ comes across the lane, X⁴ goes over the top, X² jams in and is prepared to take two passes coming out of the corner, and X⁵ plays (5). See Diagram 8-30.

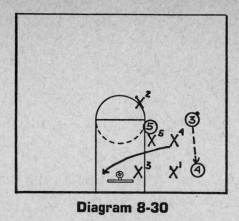

Diagram 8-30

Corner to Side to Front

X³ and X⁴ have again changed sides, X¹ slides to the ballside lane, and X² takes both passes. See Diagrams 8-31 and 8-32.

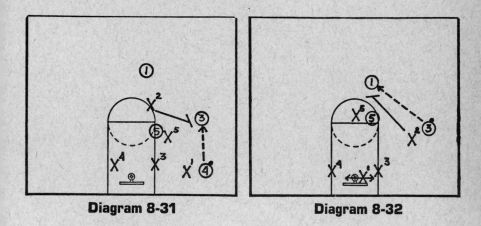

Diagram 8-31   **Diagram 8-32**

Even to Odd

Many teams start with two guards and cut one through against zones. When this happens, X¹ and X² match the two offensive guards and X¹ goes through with the cutter and then covers both corners. See Diagram 8-33. In effect, he has become the Monster.

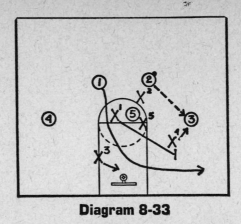

Diagram 8-33

From here, the same slides are used as those used against odd-man fronts.

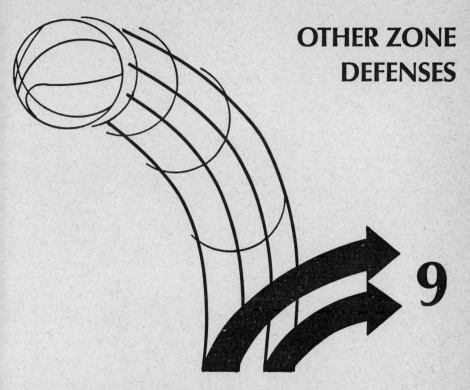

OTHER ZONE DEFENSES

9

The following zone defenses can be used to cover both odd and even front offensive perimeters. They are best used as supplements to the teams basic defense or as defenses to meet specific situations.

THE 2-3 CHECK ZONE

The check zone is designed to keep the three rebounders, X^3, X^4, and X^5, close to the basket. It puts added pressure on the defensive two-front man, but results in better rebounding position without sacrificing coverage. It is not a zone that provides many opportunities for interceptions. Although it is a 2-3 zone, it may be used successfully against both even and odd front zone offenses.

Versus Even Front Offenses

Front

As the two offensive guards bring the ball upcourt, they are met by X^2. X^1 plays behind X^2 at the free-throw line area, cheating slightly toward the ballside. X^2 attempts to turn the guard with the ball (1) and induce him to throw it to the wing man on his side (3). The back three defenders at this time each have at least one foot in the lane. See Diagram 9-1.

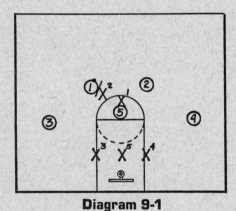

Diagram 9-1

Side

When (1) does pass to his wing man (3), X^1 quickly moves over to cover. X^3, X^5, and X^4 stay in the lane unless there is a man in the ballside corner. This isn't very likely when the offense has a two-man front, but when it does occur, X^3 moves one-third of the way to the corner. This causes X^5 to move to within eight feet of X^3, and X^4 within eight feet of X^5. X^2 jams the high post area. If there is a high post man, X^2 should front him and touch him while doing so. See Diagram 9-2.

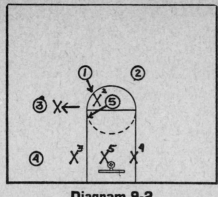

Diagram 9-2

Corner

If the pass is made to the corner, X^3 covers with X^5 trailing him by eight feet, and X^4 trailing X^5 by eight feet. X^1 tries to get his head between (3) and the ball. See Diagram 9-3.

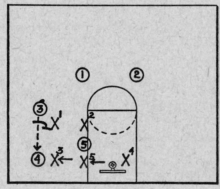

Diagram 9-3

Out of Corner Side

Once the ball gets to the corner, X^1 knows he must cover the next two perimeter passes coming out. So if the ball is passed from the offensive man in the corner to (3), and then to (1), X^1 must cover both (3) and (1). While X^1 is doing this difficult job, X^2 must protect for him and make sure neither (3) nor (1) penetrates on a dribble. See Diagrams 9-4 and 9-5.

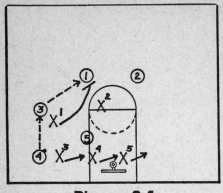

Diagram 9-4

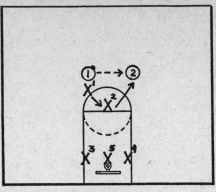

Diagram 9-5

Second Side

The defensive maneuvers up to this point are called "the first side." Once the ball has been reversed, a defensive adjustment called "second side" must be made.

When the ball is reversed by way of the offside guard to the offside forward (4), the defensive wing on that side, X^4, must come up and check him until X^2 gets there. See Diagram 9-6. As soon as X^2 arrives, X^4 releases and drops back to the lane. If there is a man in the corner, X^4 moves one-third of the way to the corner and is prepared to approach the corner in a manner that denies a baseline drive. See Diagram 9-7.

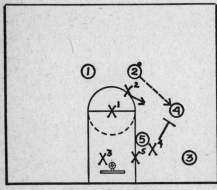

Diagram 9-6

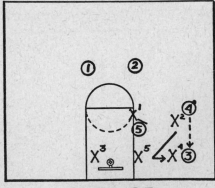

Diagram 9-7

Out of Corner

When the ball comes out of the corner, X^2 must be prepared to cover the first two perimeter passes as X^1 did on the first side. At the time the ball is coming out of the corner and is to be passed from wing to front, the protecting guard (X^1 in Diagram 9-8) should watch the position of the guard receiving the pass to the front. If (2) moves toward (4) to shorten the distance of the pass, it will make it easy for X^2 to cover.

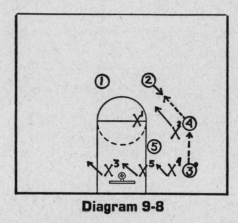

Diagram 9-8

If (2) does not move toward (4), it might be wise for X^1 to attempt to intercept this long pass, which has a bad angle. See Diagram 9-9.

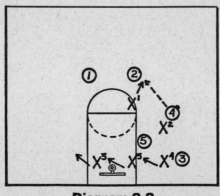

Diagram 9-9

Pass to Post

Any time a pass is made to the post, the middle man, X^5, must cover it and the two back wings, X^3 and X^4, must pinch. See Diagram 9-10.

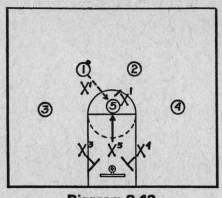

Diagram 9-10

Versus Odd Front Zones

Front to Side

As the ball comes upcourt, it is again met by X^2. X^2 tries to force the point man (1) in a given direction and have him pass to the wing man on that side. X^1 starts at the free-throw line, cheats toward the side the ball is being forced to, and covers the first wing pass. As soon as the pass to the wing man (2) is made, X^2 flattens out and jams the high post area. See Diagram 9-11.

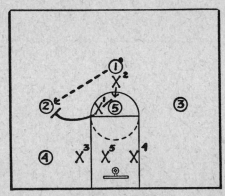

Diagram 9-11

Side to Corner

If the next pass is to the corner, X^3 covers it, X^1 pressures (2), and X^2 is ready to protect. See Diagram 9-12.

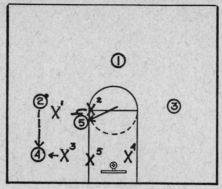

Diagram 9-12

Out of the Corner

As the ball comes out of the corner, X^1 knows he must cover the two perimeter passes again. Once the ball gets to the side, X^2 should notice if (1) moves to meet (2)'s pass. If he does, X^1's job is fairly easy. See Diagram 9-13. If not, X^2 should go for the interception. See Diagram 9-14.

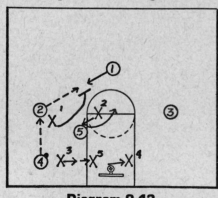

Diagram 9-13

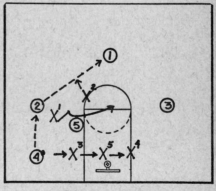

Diagram 9-14

Second Side

Once the ball gets to the point and is then reversed to (3), the back wing man on that side, X^4, must move up and check (3) until X^2 gets there, and then drop back. See Diagram 9-15.

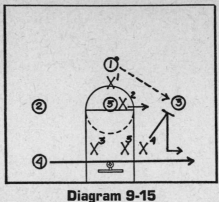

Diagram 9-15

X^4 is then in position to cover the corner pass.

Pass to Post

When the ball is passed to the post versus a one-man front, X^5 still covers it and the two back wing men pinch. See Diagram 9-16.

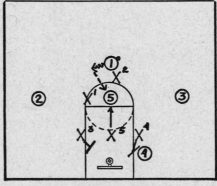

Diagram 9-16

This zone is ideal for teams with quick guards and big rebounders in the back positions. It is particularly functional if middle man X^5 is big and strong and can dominate the boards because he never leaves the pivot area.

THE TALL POINT MAN ZONE

This zone necessitates having a tall, agile point man, X^1.

Versus an Odd Front

Front

When the offense plays an odd front, point man X¹ covers the offensive point man. See Diagram 9-17.

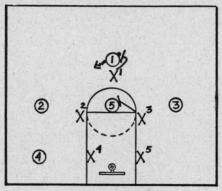

Diagram 9-17

Diagram 9-17 also shows X¹ forcing (1) to one side. This allows the offside wing, X³, to jam the high post area.

Side

As the ball is passed to the offensive wing man (2), X², the defensive wing man on that side, must cover him. Point man X¹ must make a deep drop on this pass, which leaves him inside the free-throw line. The ballside back man, X⁴, then looks to the corner. If there is an offensive man in the corner, he moves one-third of the way toward him. See Diagram 9-18.

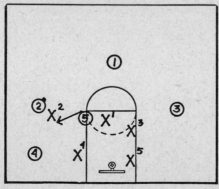

Diagram 9-18

If there is no man in the corner, X^4 stays with one foot in the lane. See Diagram 9-19.

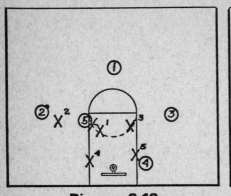

Diagram 9-19

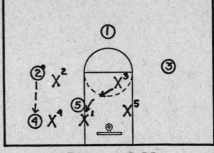

Diagram 9-20

Corner

When the ball is passed to the corner, as shown in Diagram 9-20, X^4 covers the man with the ball, X^1 slides into the post area, and X^3 moves into the lane to form a rebounding triangle with X^1 and with X^5, who has remained in the key rebounding area (the offside lay-up slot).

Versus an Even-Man Front

If the offense has an even-man front, X^1 retreats inside the free-throw line and X^2 and X^3 cover the two offensive front men. See Diagram 9-21.

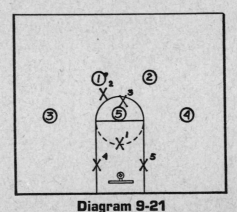

Diagram 9-21

Then as the ball is moved around the perimeter, the slides are as shown in Diagrams 9-22, 9-23, and 9-24.

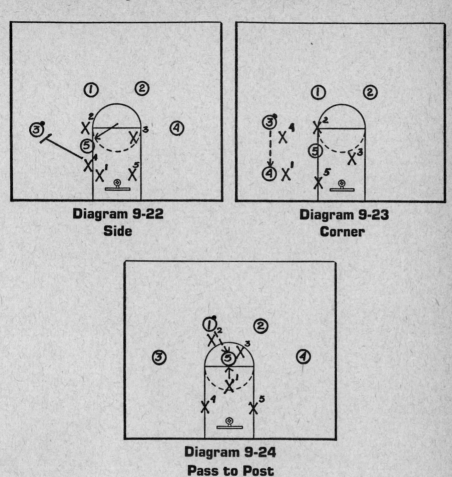

Diagram 9-22
Side

Diagram 9-23
Corner

Diagram 9-24
Pass to Post

This zone allows the defense to adjust easily to even and odd perimeters.

THE 1-3-1 ZONE

Versus an Odd Front

The 1-3-1 naturally matches an odd perimeter and allows for the easy coverage shown in Diagrams 9-25 through Diagram 9-28.

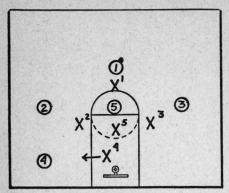

Diagram 9-25
Front

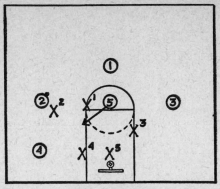

Diagram 9-26
Side

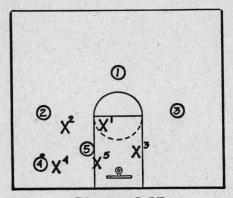

Diagram 9-27
Corner

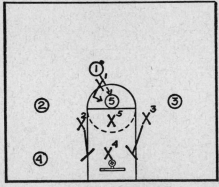

Diagram 9-28
Pass to Post

Versus an Even Front

Against an even front, the 1-3-1 zone simply double teams. Diagrams 9-29 through 9-31 show the slides.

Front

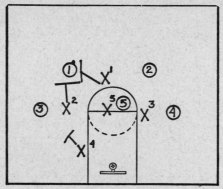

Diagram 9-29

X^1 and the ballside wing, X^2, double team.

X^3 makes a deep drop.

X^5 jams the high post area.

X^4 prepares to cover the side.

Side

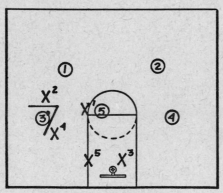

Diagram 9-30

X^1 releases and jams the high post area.

X^2 double teams behind him.

X^4 stops the ball.

X^5 prepares to cover the corner.

Corner

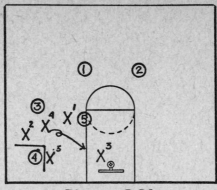

Diagram 9-31

X¹ jams the lane.

X² double teams.

X⁴ releases and hustles to cover the post.

X⁵ covers the corner.

X³ protects the basket.

This zone eliminates the problems of attempting to adjust to different perimeters. It simply takes advantage of the natural match-up of an odd front and double teams an even-fronted perimeter.

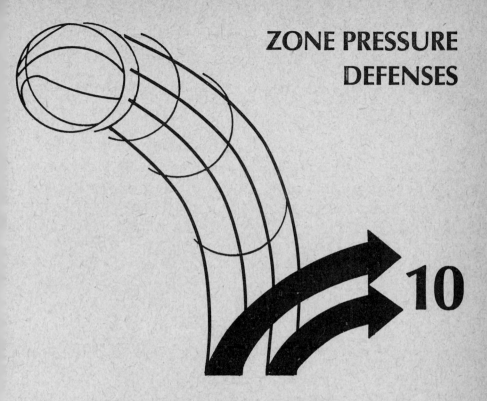

ZONE PRESSURE
DEFENSES

10

This chapter offers three zone pressure defenses. The first two are novel approaches and the third is the tried and true 1-2-1-1 press.

A TWO-FACED ZONE PRESS

One of the major weaknesses of many zone pressure defenses is that once they have been diagnosed by the offense, they are easy to penetrate. This defense presents a special problem in that it has two faces. On one side of the court it is an overplaying, almost man-to-man defense, and on the other it is an "invite the pass in and double team type" zone press.

The initial alignment of the defenders is a 1-2-1-1 shape. It consists of a front chaser, X^1, two wings, X^2 and X^3, a midcourt man, X^4, and a safety man, X^5. See Diagram 10-1.

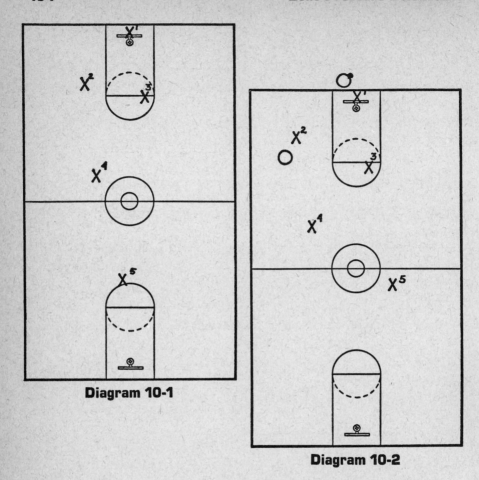

Diagram 10-1

Diagram 10-2

From this point the scouting report will come in to play. It is desirable to overplay the obvious inbounds pass receiver. It is a percentage assumption to plan on this player's being on X^2's side of the court the majority of the time. Most of the time the person making the inbounds pass will be right-handed and this tends to condition him to turn to that side. Because of this, X^2 should be a dogged defender and be assigned to overplay the obvious inbounds receiver. Also, because of this, the midcourt man is told to shade to that side of the court and play about at the ballside free-throw lane line extended. X^1, the chaser, is told to force the ball in the direction of X^2 by overplaying the inbound passer to the other side. The offside wing overshifts and plays in the lane and free-throw line high. The safety man, X^5, shades a couple of steps toward the weak side to compensate for X^4 overshift. See Diagram 10-2.

X^5 must also consider the position of the offense's deepest player. A good rule is for him to play halfway between their deep man and the midcourt line. This, of course, would vary with the ability of the inbounder to throw the long pass and the deep man's size and ability to catch it.

From here, one of two situations may occur.

1. Pass to Overplay Side

Since this pass is very often a lob pass brought on by X^2's overplay, X^4 is conditioned to move up on it, and: (a) intercept; (b) draw a step-in foul on (2), who is probably facing the passer and out of control; or (c) at least stop the progress of the ball, which will result in a double team on (2) formed by X^2 and X^4. See Diagrams 10-3 through 10-5.

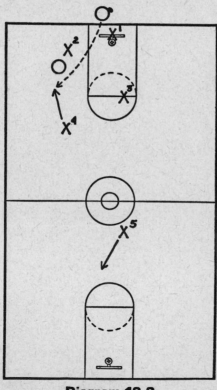

Diagram 10-3

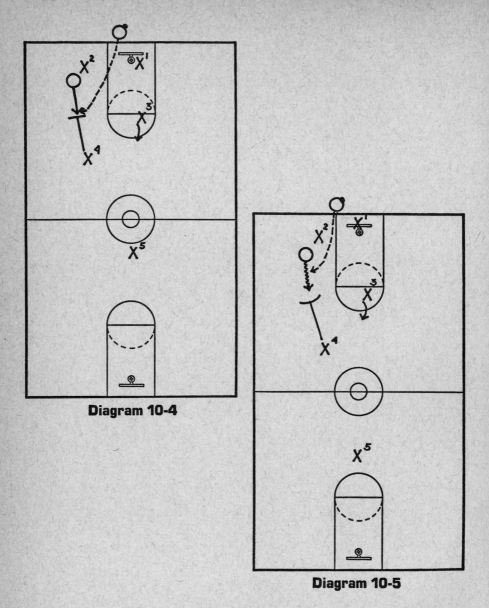

Diagram 10-4

Diagram 10-5

2. Pass to the Openside

When the inbound pass is made to X^3's side, X^3 must stop the ball and X^1 will double team. See Diagram 10-6.

Then if the ball is thrown to midcourt, X^4 will stop it and X^3 would then double team. See Diagram 10-7.

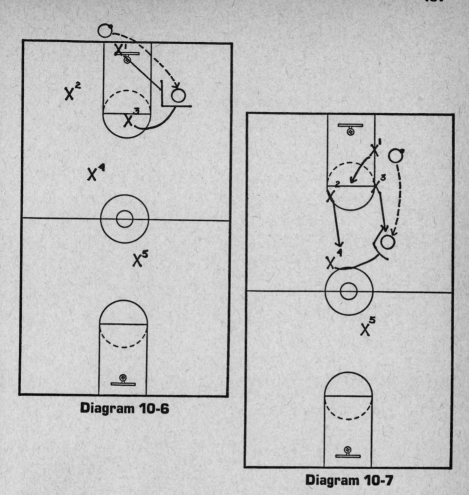

Diagram 10-6

Diagram 10-7

Thus the two faces of the press are provided by having an overplaying, forcing defense on one side and an arrangement that provides for two traps on the opposite side.

Long Passes

X^4, the midcourt man, and X^5, the safety man, must be a team. They are instructed that when a pass is made from behind the backcourt free-throw line and it goes over the head of the midcourt man, X^5 will attempt to intercept and X^4 must run for the basket. On long cross-court passes, X^5 will make the call. If he calls "Mine," X^4 must again run for the basket. See Diagram 10-8.

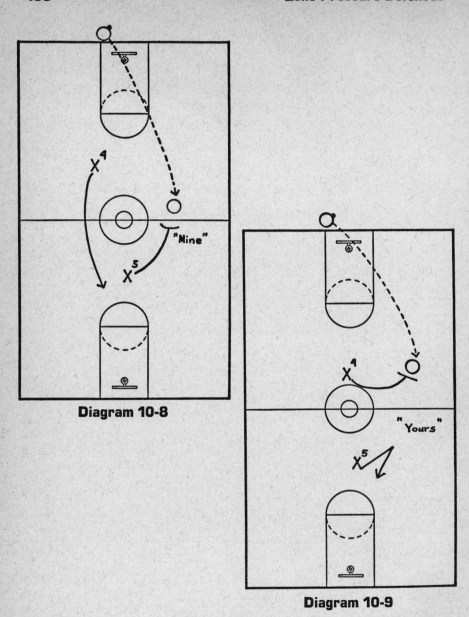

Diagram 10-8

Diagram 10-9

If X⁵ calls "Yours," X⁴ must hustle crosscourt and get to the ball. See Diagram 10-9.

Once the ball is inbounded, the defense follows general zone press rules.

X^1 Point Man	Bother the first pass in, make one double team, and retreat.
X^3 Wing Man	*Onside*—Stop the ball in front of you and double team when it goes past you on your side. *Offside*—Go to the middle and stay as high as the ball.
X^4 Midcourt Man	Intercept or stop the ball in front of you. Run for the basket when the ball goes over your head. X^5 will make a call on crosscourt passes.
X^5 Safety Man	Intercept anything thrown long from behind the far free-throw line. Make a call on crosscourt passes.
X^2 Wing Man	*Onside*—Deny the inbounds pass and double team once it is past you. *Offside*—Jam the middle and stay as high as the ball.

THE RUN AND JUMP ZONE

Although this defense is a pressure zone, it is actually a variation of the run and jump, man-to-man defense. It presents an entirely new defensive picture to the offensive players, and the results are often turnovers and confusion.

Defensive Set

The run and jump zone is run from a 2-3 zone set. After a score, the defensive team hustles back to the front court area. As the two offensive guards (1) and (2) bring the ball upcourt, the two defensive guards, X^1 and X^2, jump out at them and meet them at an area between the head of the backcourt free-throw circle and the midcourt circle. The other three defenders are lined up with a middle man, X^4, positioned to deny any passes to that area, and a wing man on each side (X^3 and X^5). See Diagram 10-10.

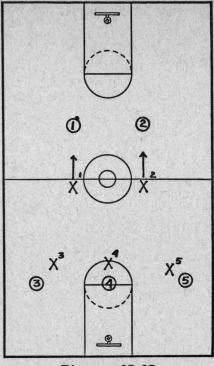

Diagram 10-10

The wing men are instructed to front the first man on their side. From here, one of two situations may occur.

Guard-to-Guard

This defensive play is called when the front defender on the ball (X^1) turns the ball inside toward the other defensive guard, X^2. He forces (1) to dribble in that direction and X^2 steps into his ((1's) path. What one can anticipate happening at this point is X^2's man, (2), sensing that he is open and cutting down the side line. (2) will be looking for a pass from (1). Because of this, the wing man on that side, X^5, moves up and may:

(A) intercept this pass (see Diagram 10-11);

(B) draw a step-in foul on (2) (see Diagram 10-12); or

(C) if he (X³) gets there late, stop (2) and make him pick up his dribble (see Diagram 10-13).

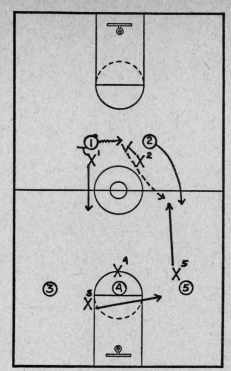

Diaram 10-11

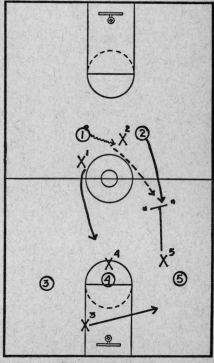

Diagram 10-12

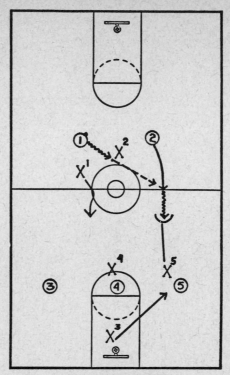

Diagram 10-13

As shown in these three diagrams, the offside wing man, X^3, must come across and cover the ballside forward (5). The defensive guard who initated the play, X^1, must run for the offside lay-up lane. In effect, a four-man defensive rotation has taken place involving X^1, X^2, X^3, and X^5. The other man, X^4, took care of his very important job of keeping the ball out of the middle.

In terms of rules, the players operated in the following manner.

X^1 *The onside guard* initiated the play, and then ran for the offside lay-up slot.

X^2 *The offside guard* stopped the ball.

X^5 *The onside wing man* came up.

X^3 *The offside wing man* came across.

X^4 *The middle man* kept the ball from getting into his area. When things break down, he also must beat the ball to the basket.

Diagram 10-14 shows the guard-to-guard defensive play being run on the opposite side of the court.

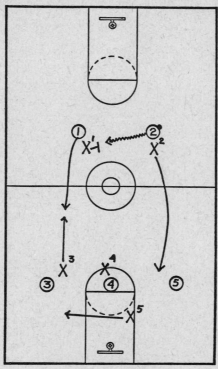

Diagram 10-14

Guard-to-Wing

This defensive play is accomplished when the onside guard (X^1 in Diagram 10-15) decides to force (1) to dribble down the side line. Again, the rules are followed: the onside wing man (X^3 in Diagram 10-15) comes up, and the offside wing man X^5 comes across. The initiating guard, X^1, runs for the offside lay-up slot, and the middle man, X^4, prevents the ball from coming into the lane area extended. See Diagram 10-15.

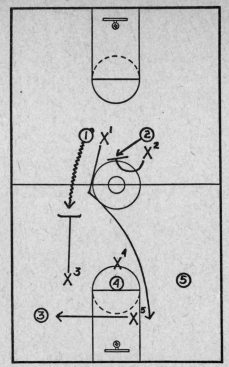

Diagram 10-15

X^3's instructions are to make (1) pick up his dribble, or, if he is out of control, draw a step-in foul on him. X^2 stays with (2), so this play is a three-man rotation.

The basic plan of both of these defensive plays is to force the man with the ball to dribble and, if possible, get him out of control. From there, someone will step out on him and get him to throw a hurried pass. This pass will usually be in the direction he is moving. The two most vulnerable passes that must be emphasized are the following.

1. Guard-to-Guard

When (1) is forced to dribble inside and is stopped by the offside guard, X^2, (2) will usually move down his sideline toward the basket. The onside wing man, X^5, must be prepared to intercept the pass from (1) to (2). See Diagram 10-16.

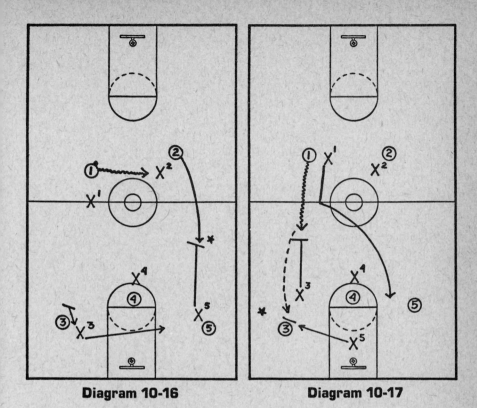

Diagram 10-16   **Diagram 10-17**

2. Guard-to-Forward

When (1) is forced to dribble down the sideline by X^1, X^3 must come up quickly and at least stop him. When this happens, X^5 must get across the court and intercept or at least deflect the pass from (1) to (3). See Diagram 10-17.

Two other passes that definitely must be prevented are as follows.

The Pass to the Middle

Most teams, when they feel pressure, plan to get the ball into the middle. X^4 has the all-important job of denying this.

The Long Crosscourt Pass

When this happens, there is not enough pressure up front. The front defenders, X^1 and X^2, must make the dribbler run for his life.

He should not be allowed the privilege of looking downcourt. If this pass succeeds, the offside wing man must be aware of it the next time around and go for it.

This is a bang-bang type pressure defense. After two passes are received in the front court, the team rotates to a basic 2-3 zone. This is accomplished primarily by the onside wing man, who will always be up, moving the offside wing position. See Diagrams 10-18 and 10-19.

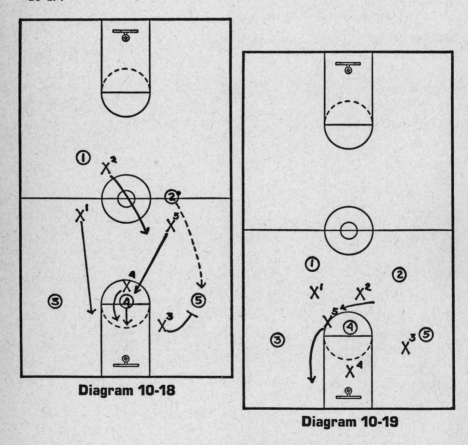

Diagram 10-18

Diagram 10-19

From there, standard 2-3 zone slides are utilized.

THE 1-2-1 ZONE PRESS

The 1-2-1-1 shape press is probably the most frequently used zone press. Its alignment facilitates many double teams and provides excellent floor coverage. It can best be taught by presenting the players the press's rules and then showing the rules in action.

Point Man—X¹

You must attempt to harass the inbound passer. You should force him to throw to the overshifted side of the press and cause him to lob the pass; if possible, you should tip the throw-in.

Once the throw-in is made, you should seal any double team that occurs prior to the backcourt free-throw line. Once the ball passes that free-throw line, run to the basket you are defending.

Wing Men—X² and X³

Onside

When the ball is on your side of the court, you attempt to stop it in front of you and double team it once it has gone by you.

Offside

Move to the middle and stay as high as the ball. You have the very important assignment of denying the pass to the middle

Front Deep—X⁴

You must cheat to the ballside and stop the ball in front of you. This requires being prepared to cover either side of the court.

If the ball goes over your head or to a deep crosscourt position, you must run to protect the basket.

Safety Man or Back Deep—X⁵

Play as high as you can without allowing a long pass for an easy basket.

Before the ball has reached the backcourt free-throw line, you must attempt to intercept any long or deep crosscourt pass. Once the ball is over that line, be more conservative and protect the basket.

When you are outnumbered and alone, retreat to the lane and protect the basket. Give them the jump shot and contest all lay-up shots. If possible, draw a step-in foul. See Diagram 10-20.

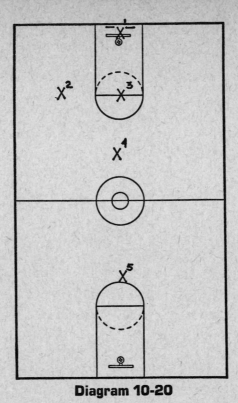

Diagram 10-20

THE RULES IN ACTION

Front

When the initial throw-in is made in front of the onside wing man (X^2 in Diagram 10-20), the following steps should be taken:

X^2 stops the ball. X^3 jams the middle.

X^1 seals the double team.

X^4 moves to the ballside.

X^5 prepares for a possible interception by observing the positions of the offensive men and watching the feet and eyes of the man with the ball.

Front to Midcourt

When the ball is then passed to the midcourt area, the following moves should be made:

X^4 stops the ball.

X^2 seals the double team.

X^3 stays as high as the ball and denies the pass to the middle.

X^5 makes sure no one is behind him.

X^1 releases and runs to protect the basket.

See Diagram 10-21

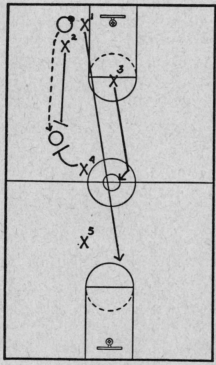

Diagram 10-21

Front to Offside Front

When this pass occurs, the former offside wing man, X^3, becomes the onside wing man and must stop the ball.

X^1 again seals the double team.

X^2 must now jam the middle, stay as high as the ball, and deny the pass to the middle.

X⁴ must move crosscourt to the new ballside and be prepared to stop the ball.

X⁵ must move slightly to the ballside.

See Diagram 10-22.

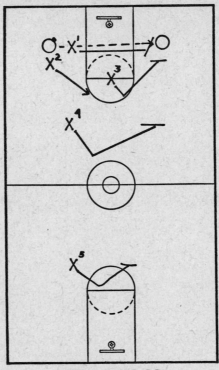

Diagram 10-22

Front to Deep

When the ball is passed from the front position and over the head of the front deep man, it is a long pass.

X⁵, the back deep or safety man, must attempt to intercept or at least stop the ball.

X⁴, the front deep man, must hustle to protect the basket.

X², the offside wing man, attempts to stay as high as the ball.

X³ runs to double team the receiver.

X¹ is released and runs for the basket.

See Diagram 10-23.

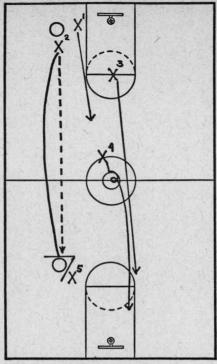

Diagram 10-23

Front to Crosscourt

Practically the same rules are followed when a long crosscourt pass is made.

X^5 must go for it.

X^4 protects for X^5.

X^3 becomes the offside wing man and moves to the middle and as high as the ball.

X^2 becomes the onside wing man and must seal the double team.

X^1 releases and runs for the basket.

The Two-Up Adjustment

When the offense places two men at midcourt and no one downcourt, the defense can play both the front deep man, X^4, and the back deep man, X^5, at midcourt on opposite sides. Then they are told if the ball comes their way, they play the front deep position and if it goes opposite them, they must play the back deep position and protect the basket.

General Pressing Rules

1. Stop the forward progress of the ball.
2. Don't run past a potential double team.
3. When double teaming, stay low until the man with the ball picks up his dribble.
4. Watch the feet and eyes of the man with the ball.
5. Be aware of the men in your area.
6. A press is a gambling defense, so go for the interception. Learn to anticipate their pattern.
7. Force the man with the ball to throw a lob pass.
8. If the dribbler is out of control, draw a step-in foul.
9. Beat the ball to the basket.
10. Get into and out of the press at the right time and as quickly as possible.

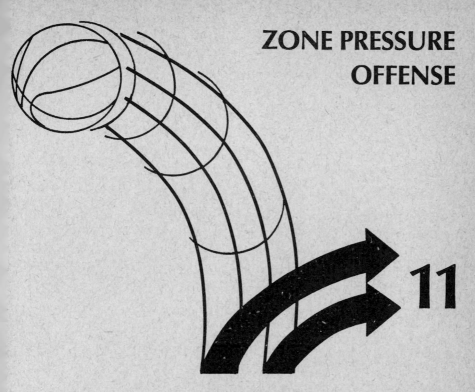

ZONE PRESSURE
OFFENSE

11

The zone pressure defense is a calculated risk at best. This point should be stressed when teaching the zone pressure offense. If the offense is aware that the opponents are attempting to cover the entire floor and that most defenses have trouble covering 30 percent of it, they may gain a psychological edge.

Show your team that if the zone press is double teaming, if the offense has elongated the press by sending a man downcourt who must be covered, and if the other offensive players are strategically placed, the odds are very much against the defense succeeding. They will be left with two defenders covering three offensive players in a fairly large area. Someone should always be open.

Next, point out the advantages of getting the ball into the middle of the press. The offensive players should be shown that the zone press cannot thoroughly cover both sides of the court. They must favor the ballside. When the ball is passed to the middle of the press, the defense must collapse on it, and this often leaves both sides of the court open. This is particularly true of the offside (the side opposite that from which the ball was passed to the middle).

The players should then be made aware of the fundamentals that are important within the context of all zone pressure offenses. Some of them are: knowing who should dribble, when, and how much; acknowledging the importance of coming to meet all passes; seeing the advantages of the two-hand overhead pass; being aware of what is happening on the entire court; sensing how long the ten-second count really is; splitting or dribbling through a double team; avoiding the step-in foul; knowing the danger of the pass across the backcourt free-throw lane; protecting the ball when double teamed; avoiding the trap areas; knowing the hazards of not moving the ball; and capitalizing on potential scoring situations.

Then the game plan in relation to the press should be spelled out to the players. Are they going to attempt to blitz the opposition's press by rushing the ball upcourt and all the way to the basket, or are they to work it methodically upcourt and set up their basic offense if an unmolested shot does not develop? The answer to this question will be determined by the personnel available, your coaching philosophy, and the strengths and weaknesses of the opposition. The plan may vary with each game, but, in general, it should conform with the overall game plan. It may not be wise to play a control offense, but to attempt to blitz the press when it is used against you. It is very difficult for many players to play at varying tempos.

Finally, specific team techniques should be presented. Some examples of these zone press breaking team techniques are as follows.

A GUARD-ORIENTED ZONE PRESS OFFENSE

The two primary components of any basketball maneuver are the play's design and the players' skills. Too often the specific abilities of the players are ignored and coaches spend their time trying to "X" and "O" their way through tough situations. The following zone press offense gives equal weight to both.

Personnel Alignment

The team's best ball handler (1) takes the ball out of bounds. The second and third most dependable pressure meeters, (2) and

(3), are stacked at the head of the backcourt key, facing the ball. The two weak players (4) and (5), are located one on each side of the court and at midcourt. See Diagram 11-1.

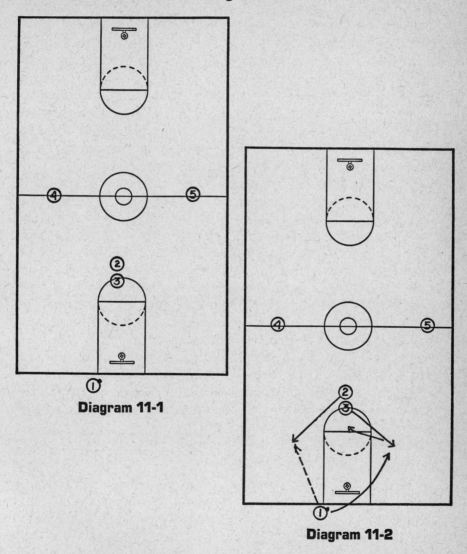

Diagram 11-1

Diagram 11-2

(2) initiates the play by cutting toward either backcourt corner. Player (3) then goes toward the corner opposite (2). (1) may pass to either (2) or (3). In Diagram 11-2, (1) passes to (2). When this happens, (3) cuts to the middle and (1) replaces him.

From here, the following guard-oriented options may be run.

A. Pass to the Middle

(2) passes to (3) in the middle and the ball is quickly reversed to (1). This catches the zone press overshifted to (2)'s side and permits (1) to dribble upcourt. See Diagram 11-3.

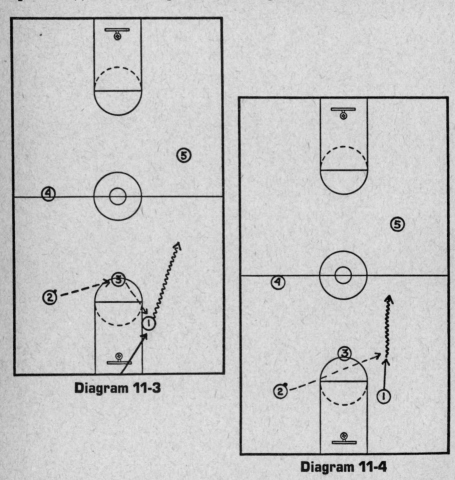

Diagram 11-3

Diagram 11-4

B. Crosscourt Lob to (1)

This, in effect, is the same play as Option A, but the pass to the middle is eliminated and (2) simply lobs crosscourt to (1), who brings it upcourt. See Diagram 11-4.

C. Pass Back to (1) and a Fake Reverse

In this option, (2) quickly returns the ball to (1), who then passes to (3) in the middle. (1) then hesitates as (3) fakes to (2), pulling the zone in that direction. (3) then passes back to (1) moving upcourt. See Diagram 11-5 and Diagram 11-6.

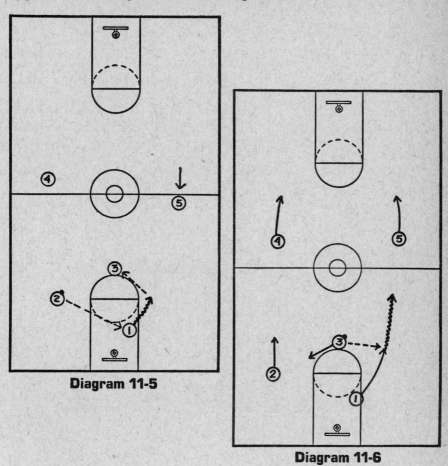

Diagram 11-5

Diagram 11-6

(4) and (5) are told to move toward the ball when it is on their side, to go to the backcourt when it is opposite them, and to run for their basket when it appears the ball has penetrated the press.

All three of the options are based on the same premises: (1) is a great ball handler; (2) and (3) are adequate; and if (4) and (5) must handle the ball to any great extent, the team is in trouble.

AN ALL-PURPOSE FULL COURT PRESS PATTERN

It is not a rare game in today's basketball when a team will face both zone and man-to-man full court pressure. This press pattern may be used against either. It allows a team to inbounds the ball, get it upcourt, and, if the defense does not recover quickly, score.

Versus Man-to-Man Pressure

The initial personnel alignment is a stack at the head of the key featuring the two guards (1) and (2), plus the tallest forward (4). The smaller, better ball-handling forward (3), takes it out-of-bounds and center streaks for the far end looking for a long pass and an easy score. See Diagram 11-7.

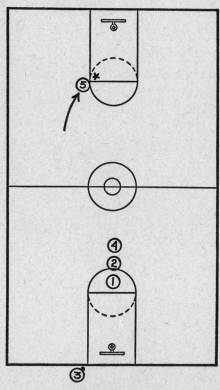

Diagram 11-7

As (3) bounces the ball, it keys the front guard (1) to break to one of the corners looking for a pass from (3). Many defensive teams will overplay this cut in a very strong manner. Some defenders will stay between the ball and the man. The second man in line, (2), will fake in (1)'s direction and cut to the opposite corner. He also will be strongly overplayed. (4) will break directly ahead. He will probably have a taller, slower player on him and the pressure will not be as great. See Diagram 11-8.

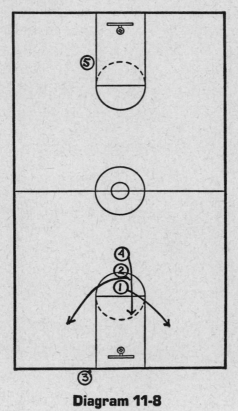

Diagram 11-8

From here, two options may be run.

I. Pass to Side

When (3) passes to either guard at the side, he slash cuts off the middle man (4) looking for a return pass, and then cuts to the ballside midcourt area. See Diagram 11-9.

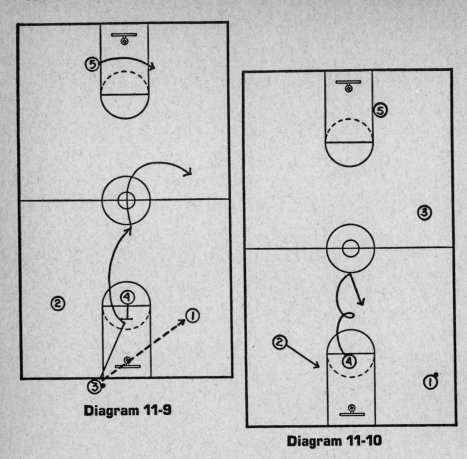

Diagram 11-9

Diagram 11-10

(4) then rolls to the area between the two backcourt circles and (1) and (2) bring the ball upcourt using him as a safety valve. See Diagram 11-10.

2. Pass to the Middle

As (1) and (2) cut to their corners, they are usually strongly overplayed by their defenders. When the ball is inbounded from (3) to (4) in the middle, both side men backdoor their defenders and are very often able to take a pass and organize a fast break by dribbling to the middle. The big man downcourt is told to fill the lane the guard took the pass in, and the offside guard fills the other. See Diagram 11-11.

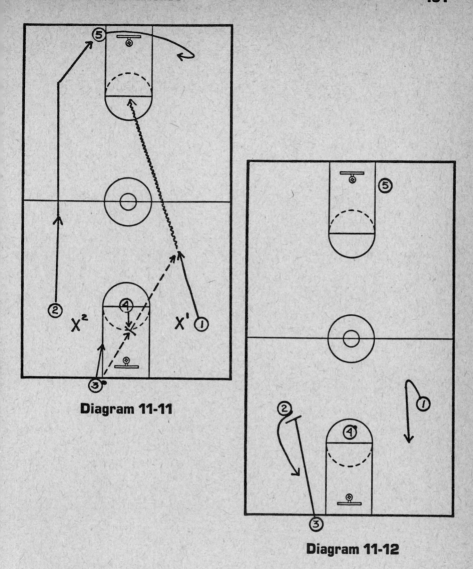

Diagram 11-11

Diagram 11-12

If neither (1) nor (2) is open on his backdoor cut, (3) makes his usual cut and stops at the head of the backdoor key. Both (1) and (2) come back to the ball with (2) using (3) to get open. See Diagram 11-12.

(4) cuts to the area between the two backcourt circles, (3) rolls to his midcourt ballside area, and (1) and (2) bring the ball upcourt with (4)'s help when needed. See Diagram 11-13.

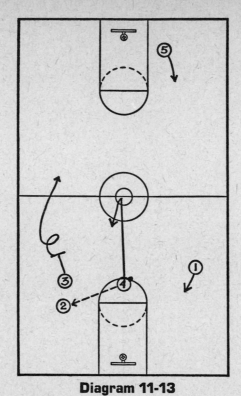

Diagram 11-13

It should be noted that very often the initial phases of this offense are enough. Either the guards will get open on their backdoor cuts when the ball is passed to the middle, or the slash cutter will get open on a pass to the sides.

Versus Zone Defense

The same initial alignment is kept and the original cuts put much pressure on the full court zone pressure defense. They must cover each of the corners plus the middle. Most zone pressing defenses can't do this.

Pass to Side

When the ball is inbounded to a side, (3) makes his normal cut and then goes to the midcourt ballside area. (1) can now look for (4) in the middle, for (3) at midcourt, or (2) crosscourt. See Diagrams 11-14 and 11-15.

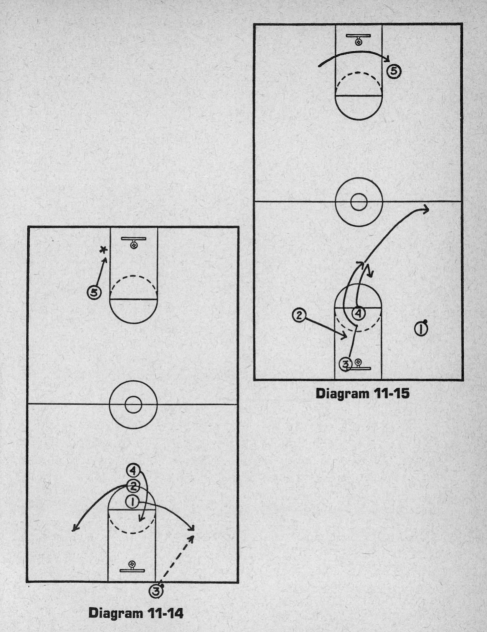

Diagram 11-15

Diagram 11-14

From there on, (4) and (3) take turns in the middle following this rule: if the ball is on your side, you are on that sideline; if the ball is on the other side, you have the middle. So on a pass from (1) to (2), their movement would be as shown in Diagram 11-16.

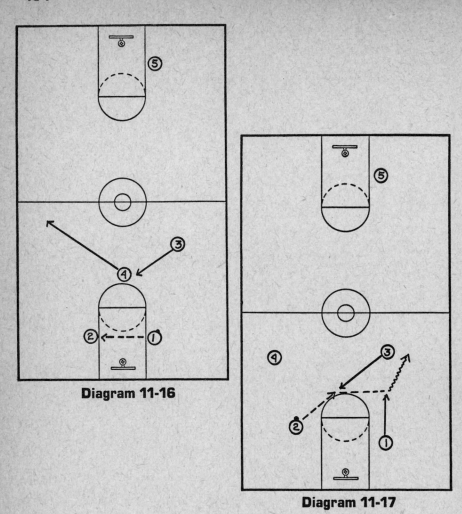

Diagram 11-16

Diagram 11-17

Anytime the ball is passed in the middle, the middle man would attempt to get it to the offside guard, who would bring it upcourt. See Diagram 11-17.

At all times (5) must stay downcourt to keep the five-zone pressure spread out.

Pass to Middle

When the pass is made inbounds in the middle to (4), both guards again backdoor and one should be open. The zone press cannot cover the middle and both sides. This is especially true when the defense is double teaming. See Diagram 11-18.

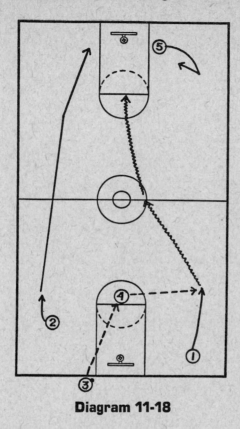

Diagram 11-18

When the defense is using changing or multiple defenses, the best rule to follow is this: when they are double teaming, get the ball in the middle and then to the weak side. If they are man-on-man, the guards must expect to bring the ball upcourt with some help from (4).

THE 2-1-2 ZONE PRESS PATTERN

In his book *Power Basketball*, Ed Jucker presented both a half court zone press pattern and a full court zone press pattern. We adopted the half court pattern and used it against all zone presses regardless of their depth. Following is the way we taught it.

Personnel Alignment

When using this pattern versus full court zone presses, the post man (5) starts at the head of the backcourt key. The two guards (1) and (2) make the inbounds play. The ballside forward (3) in Diagram 11-19 is in the backcourt and the offside forward (4) is in the front court.

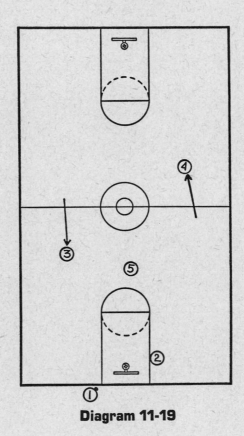

Diagram 11-19

The Guard-to-Guard Pass

The main object of this pattern is to get the ball to (5) in the middle of the press. The second goal is to pass to the onside forward (3). In this case, neither of these passes is possible so a guard (1)-to-guard (2) pass is made. As (2) receives the ball, his onside forward

(4) moves toward him and into the backcourt. The now offside forward (3) moves downcourt. (5) moves a couple of steps toward the ball and makes a jump stop in a crouched position with his elbows out. (1), of course, moves inbounds. These same moves on each guard-to-guard pass. See Diagram 11-20.

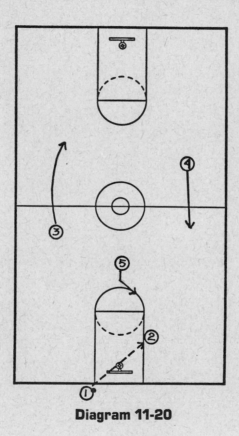

Diagram 11-20

Guard-to-Post Pass

In Diagram 11-21, guard (2) is able to get the ball to (5) in the middle. When this happens, the other guard ((1) in this case) is usually open breaking down the weak side because the zone press was overloaded on (2)'s side. (5) looks first for (1) on the weak side. He is very often open.

If (1) is not open, (5) looks downcourt for (3) or (4), who releases when the ball goes to the middle. If none of these options is open, (5) passes to (2), who is the safety man. See Diagram 11-22.

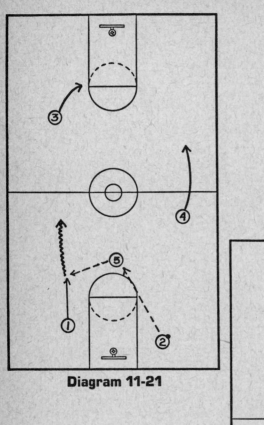

Diagram 11-21

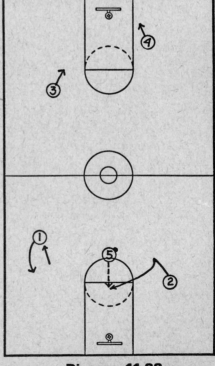

Diagram 11-22

(5) then cuts to midcourt, and (3), (4), and (1) come back to their respective positions. See Diagram 11-23.

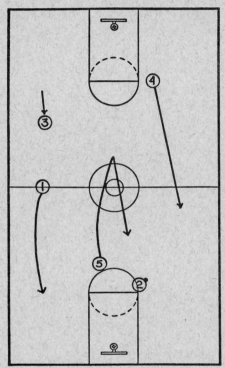

Diagram 11-23

Guard-to-Forward-to-Post Play

When a forward receives the ball, as did (4) in Diagram 11-24, the idea is still to get the ball into the middle. To facilitate this, the post man (5) cuts to the ball and makes a jump stop. When forward (4) passes to him, the offside guard (1) again cuts down the weak side and is the first option.

(5) would again look first for (1), then for the two forwards who released and went downcourt when the ball went to the middle. (2) is again the safety man. See Diagram 11-25.

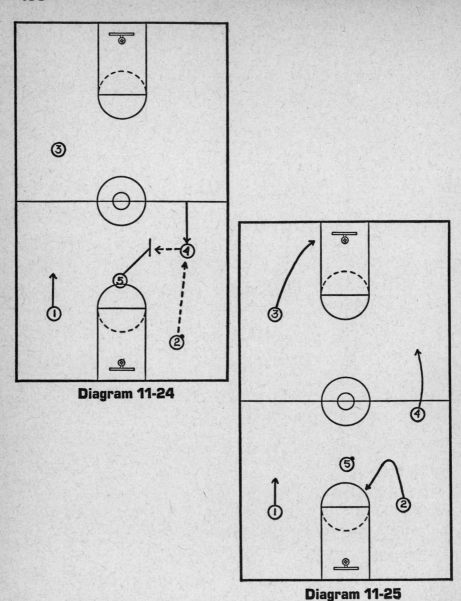

Diagram 11-24

Diagram 11-25

Crosscourt Pass

Some teams have success throwing a crosscourt guard-to-guard pass. This works because when one guard has the ball, he is usually double teamed and this leaves the offside guard open on the weak side. See Diagram 11-26.

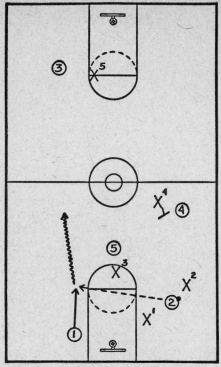

Diagram 11-26

The Pattern by Rules

Guards—Onside

Try to get the ball into the middle, and then look for the onside forward. If neither is open, make a guard-to-guard pass. You also must always be aware of your deep man (the offside forward).

Guards—Offside

When the ball goes to the middle, cut downcourt and expect to receive a pass.

Forwards—Offside

Play up in the backcourt.

Forwards—Onside

Play in the front court. When you receive the ball, look for the middle man.

Postman in Middle

Move toward the ball and jump stop in a crouched position. When you receive the ball, look to the weak side, then downcourt, and then to the safety man. Don't get too close to the man with the ball.

Rules for All

1. Move the ball.
2. Know your passing options.
3. Ten Seconds is a long time.
4. Jump balls are better than lost balls.
5. When trapped, use the two-hand overhead pass.
6. See the entire court.
7. Get the ball into the middle.
8. Dribble only as a last resort.
9. Move toward the ball when receiving it.
10. Follow the team plan once the ball gets into the front court. (Either set up or take it to the hoop.)

THE OUT OF BOUNDS
ZONE GAME

12

It is becoming an accepted practice to play zone against teams taking the ball out of bounds underneath their own basket. This practice minimizes the effectiveness of many out of bounds plays and provides the best coverage in the high percentage shooting area of the free-throw lane. This chapter concerns both the offensive and defensive phases of the out of bounds zone game.

DEFENSE

The primary goal of defending an out of bounds play is, of course, to stop the opponent from scoring. This involves two things: (a) putting pressure on the ball, and (b) jamming the free-throw lane. Following are three methods that accomplish each of these two objectives in varying degrees.

1. Jam the Middle

Alignment

The best way to jam the middle is to put all five players in the lane in a 2-3 zone formation. The three inside big men (X^3, X^4, and X^5) as shown in Diagram 12-1, should have their arms up. Their upper arms should be parallel with the floor. They should be attempting to take as much room as possible and should split their vision between the ball and the next probable cutter to their area. Each is responsible for the area found between himself and the next defensive man toward the ball. The far big man, X^4, must also be aware that many teams plan to throw to the weak side.

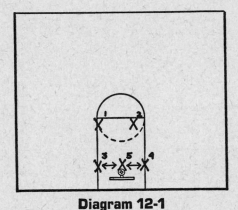

Diagram 12-1

As shown in Diagram 12-1, the two high men, X^1 and X^2, are also in the lane. X^1, the nearer of the two toward the ball, is on the near lane line and the other, X^2, is in the middle of the lane, just inside the free-throw line.

This method practically assures completion of a pass to the perimeter players. Because of this fact, the defensive players must be prepared to make the initial approach to the ball without opening up the center of the zone. This can be done by reminding the trailing inside men to stay within eight feet of the inside man ahead of him. The front men must be reminded that they must move out to the ball when it is on their side, but, more importantly, they must jam the lane when the ball goes opposite them. See Diagram 12-2.

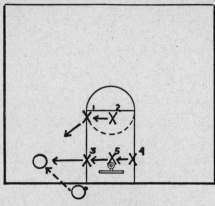

Diagram 12-2

2. Overshift Alignment

This plan gives better coverage on the perimeter but will open up the lane to a certain degree. The players line up halfway to the nearest area they are assigned to cover when the ball is in the corner. See Diagram 12-3.

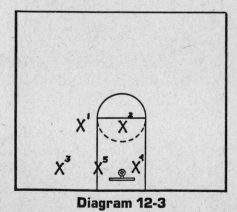

Diagram 12-3

Note that X^2 plays a little deeper and X^4 plays closer to the baseline to discourage the pass to the weak side.

3. Guarding the Inbounds Passer

This method, of course, puts pressure on the inbounds passer, but weakens the defense both on the perimeter and in the lane. See Diagram 12-4.

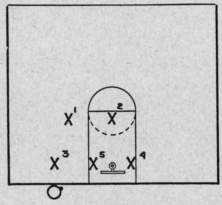

Diagram 12-4

Which is the best of the three methods? It depends on the personnel match-ups. If the offense is stronger than the defensive team inside, the defense should jam the middle. If they are a great perimeter shooting team, the defense should overshift to get quick coverage. If they are weak ball handlers and the defense has a player adept at bothering the inbounds pass, they should guard the inbounder. If the offensive team is superior in all phases, the defense should jam the middle and hope they have a bad night from the perimeter.

ZONE PLAY COMPONENTS

What sorts of movement can be expected? What do teams attempt to do against zones on out of bounds plays? Following are some of the out of bounds components used against zones.

Spread

They may make some sort of team movement that spreads the zone out (especially on the baseline). Then they may attempt to pass inside for a power lay-up. See Diagram 12-5.

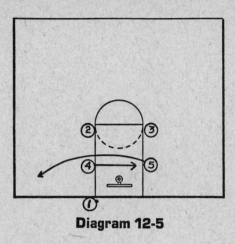

Diagram 12-5

Penetrate

After they spread the zone, they may slide people down into the low post areas. See Diagram 12-6.

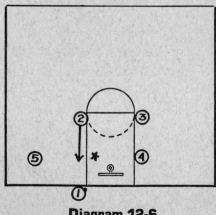

Diagram 12-6

Screen

They may screen in order to impede the progress of the lead or trailing inside man. See Diagrams 12-7 and 12-8.

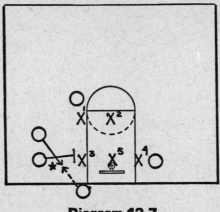

Diagram 12-7

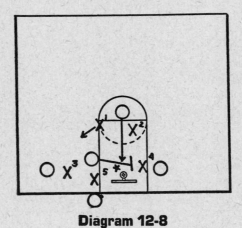

Diagram 12-8

Reverse Around the Horn

Many teams throw the ball in on one side and then reverse it quickly around the horn to catch the defense overshifted. Very often they will screen the overshift. See Diagrams 12-9 and 12-10.

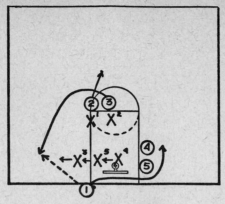

Diagram 12-9

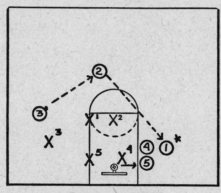

Diagram 12-10

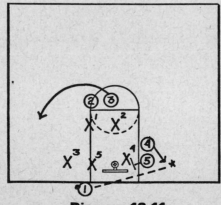

Diagram 12-11

Quick Pass to Weak Side

This works best against defensive teams that start in an overshift. The inbounder simply loops the ball to the weak side. See Diagram 12-11.

Lob Pass

Some teams have leapers or big men capable of catching a lob pass in the center of the lane and powering up for two. The defensive team must be aware of this. See Diagram 12-12.

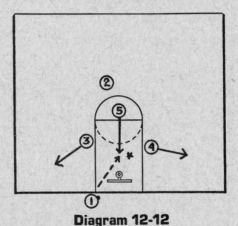

Diagram 12-12

Defensing Specific Zone Plays

These can be discovered only through scouting. Once they are known, slight adjustments can be made, but the team must still be cognizant of all potential zone out of bounds play components.

A summary of what must be involved when using zones against out of bounds plays would be to decide on the sum of the personnel match-ups, then brief the defense on the basic zone out of bounds play components, and, finally, use the scouting report to make specific adjustments to the plays you anticipate they will run.

OFFENSE OUT OF BOUNDS PLAY
VERSUS ZONE DEFENSES

An out of bounds play should provide a sure method of getting the ball inbounds and should have some scoring options. The following plays meet those requirements against zone defenses.

The Zone Spreader

This play begins from a box formation. Knowing the zone is designed to jam the middle, this play is an attempt to spread the zone and then penetrate it. The play begins when the offside deep man (5) cuts over the ballside deep man (4) and to the ballside corner. The ballside deep man (4) has instructions to let the first defender through to cover the corner, but to set a definite screen on the trailing defender by stepping into the lane. See Diagrams 12-13 and 12-14.

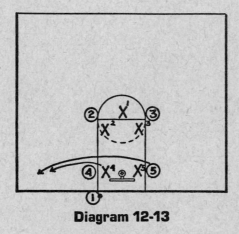

Diagram 12-13

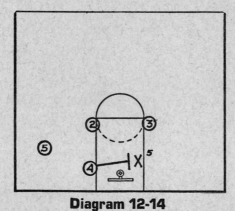

Diagram 12-14

If X^4 and X^5 are split, (2) slides down into the hole for a power lay-up shot. See Diagram 12-15.

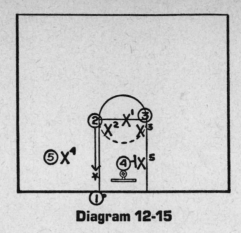

Diagram 12-15

If (1) chooses to pass to (5), he then goes opposite his pass. (5) may shoot or pass to (3), who has cut to the point. See Diagram 12-16.

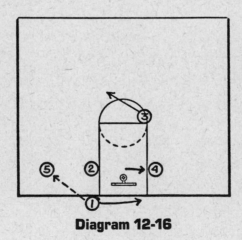

Diagram 12-16

Note in Diagram 12-16 that (4) has cleared the three-second area.

After (5) passes to (3), both he and (2) screen down for (4), who doubled back across the lane. (3) then fakes to (1) and passes to (4) behind the double screen. See Diagram 12-17.

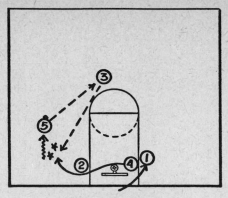

Diagram 12-17

Horizontal Stack Play

This play begins with players (2), (3), and (4) in a line, parallel with and above the free-throw line. (1) is at the head of the key, and the center (5) is taking the ball out of bounds. (1) changes directions and cuts to the ballside corner, and (4) moves to the far corner. See Diagram 12-18.

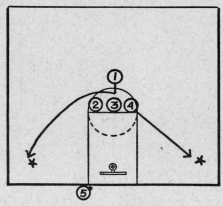

Diagram 12-18

(5) can now pass the ball to either side. In Diagram 12-19, (5) passes to (1). This tells the far man of the two remaining players at the free-throw line, (3), to move to the head of the key. (1) then

passes to (3), who fakes to (4). This fake tends to further spread the zone, since one zone player had moved out to cover (1).

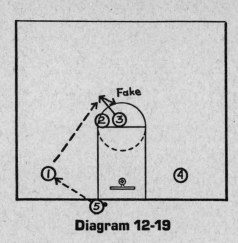

Diagram 12-19

(3) then passes to (2) at the free-throw line, and (2) turns to face the basket. This pulls the zone's middle man up to cover and leaves (5), who has stepped inbounds, open under the basket. See Diagram 12-20.

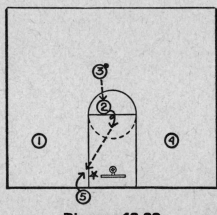

Diagram 12-20

The Double Down Play

This play is run from a box formation. It begins when (4), the inside man on the ballside, backs out to the corner. As soon as this move is made, the two top men, (2) and (3), slide into their respective lay-up areas in an attempt to catch the zone spread out. See Diagram 12-21.

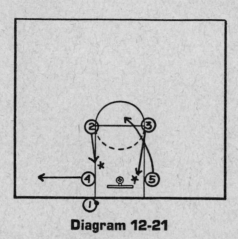

Diagram 12-21

(5), the initial far inside man, moves to the point and, if possible, uses (3) as a screen. The ball is then passed to (4) (if (2) or (3) are not open). (4) passes to (5) at the point and (1) goes opposite his pass and brushes closely by (3). See Diagram 12-22.

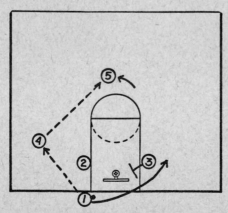

Diagram 12-22

(5) may now pass to (1) coming around (3) or fake to (1) and wait for (4) to pinch down for (2) in an attempt to catch the zone shifted toward (1)'s side. See Diagram 12-23.

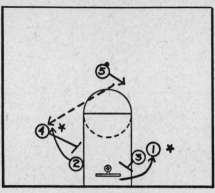

Diagram 12-23

Another option that occurs frequently is facilitated by the fact that (5) is a tall inside man and can see to pass over the smaller outside defenders. During the wide motion of (1) cutting to one side and (2) cutting to the other, the defenders, in an attempt to cover them, sometimes neglect the inside men, (3) and (4). When this happens, (5) throws a quick two-hand overhead pass to the open inside man, who shoots a power lay-up. See (4) in Diagram 12-24.

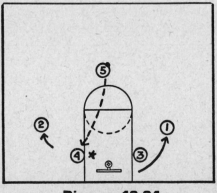

Diagram 12-24

INDEX